LEGEND & LORE OF THE
LOST ADAMS

LEGEND & LORE OF THE
LOST ADAMS

John LeMay

DEAD HORSE HISTORY

A SUBSIDIARY OF BICEP BOOKS. ROSWELL, NEW MEXICO

Printed in the United States of America

LeMay, John.
Legend & Lore of the Lost Adams
ISBN 978-1-953221-19-3
New Mexico—Treasure/Folklore/Apache

For Jason Garcia,
with whom I've wandered the scorching deserts of New Mexico

Low Falls

Aquellos dos Piloncillos

Tres Stumps

Ruins of Cabin
GOLD IS BURIED HERE

"Secret Door"

MALPAIS

The Pumpkin Patch

Sno-Ta-Hay Canyon
ALSO CALLED Z CANYON, ZIG
ZAG CANYON, GOLD CANYON,
ADAMS DIGGINGS CANYON &
HIDDEN BOX CANYON, AS
DESCRIBED BY SURVIVORS
OF APACHE ATTACK.

A NOTE FROM THE AUTHOR

"Each decade has added its chapter to the history of the lost Adams diggings, written sometimes with blood, always with tears."—
El Paso Herald, *July 2, 1927*

A s a Lost Adams enthusiast, it is not my goal to simply paraphrase and regurgitate J. Frank Dobie's *Apache Gold & Yaqui Silver* whilst adding nothing new to the legend. Nor is it this book's purpose to point you in the direction of the actual diggings. No, like my book *Tall Tales and Half Truths of Billy the Kid*, which emphasized myth and falsehood over truth, this title aims to wrangle together the most fantastic, forgotten minutia of the Adams legend. And on the note of Billy the Kid, I might as well confess that this book serves a double purpose. As of this writing, I'm composing a novel that leans heavily on the Lost Adams entitled *Billy the Kid & the Boy Bandit King*, wherein the titular outlaw crosses paths with Old Man Adams and a treasure hunt ensues. As I was researching the diggings for the novel, it struck me that I could turn my notes into a book of their own, so here it is. And yes, I suppose you could claim my book is old wine in a new bottle, but I promise you, it's very rare old wine. Actually, the research process in compiling this book was a bit like panning for gold. As I sifted through a multitude of sources, ranging from out-of-print books to long-forgotten newspaper articles, every now and again, I'd come across a piece of information that was pure gold. It will probably be the same for many of you reading this book. You likely already know the Adams legend by heart and are just "panning" for gold in the form of forgotten anecdotes and overlooked details of the diggings. So, I hope this book will turn up a few useful nuggets of new information for my fellow armchair prospectors.

John LeMay

"The lost Adams Diggings? Say, I've read all them books about the lost Adams Diggings and I tell you this is it. Now if I just had a little grub stake so I could work it right—say, we'd all be rich."
Pinos Altos, New Mexico, c.1940 (Library of Congress, Russell Lee)

TABLE OF CONTENTS

'Rattlesnake Culture' Another Dobie Idea

Deliver him from the artist who draws a green poodle dog's track and says it's a cottonwood tree, said J. Frank Dobie, left, to Tom Lea Jr., right, illustrator of Mr. Dobie's book, "Apache Gold and Yaqui Silver."

J. Frank Dobie, who brought the Adams myth to the broader public, with illustrator Tom Lea Jr. in the *El Paso Herald Post* of April 10, 1939.

INTRODUCTION
GENESIS OF THE LEGEND

The story of the Lost Adams Diggings has become legend in New Mexico and Arizona. As you no doubt already know, it tells of a procession of miners in the 1860s who stumble upon a lost canyon of gold on the New Mexico-Arizona border only to be massacred by the Apache. Of the few people to survive, and although his account is not the most reliable, the man known only as Adams emerges as the central figure of the myth. Perhaps that's because, unlike his brethren, Adams spent the rest of his days wandering the West and telling his lost gold tale in every saloon he could. In the old days, this is exactly how the story was spread; that being directly from Adams or one of his disciples.

The most traditional Adams account, in fact, a pastiche, was published by the great Texas folklorist J. Frank Dobie in his now classic work *Apache Gold & Yaqui Silver*. And, if you know Dobie, he was the first to admit that he valued a good story over hard facts. Renowned historian Marc Simmons knew this well, and in his book *Treasure Trails of the Southwest*, surmised, "I found that Mr. Dobie had taken a hodgepodge of conflicting details [about the Lost Adams] and ironed them out to make a smooth and connected story."[1]

One of the more popular portraits of J. Frank Dobie in his later years.

Modern-day prospector Jack Purcell also caught on to this, stating in his book *The Lost Adams Diggings: Myth, Mystery and Madness*:

> My first hint that the story was a lot more complex than Dobie suggested came when I began examining his bibliography and contacted the *El Paso Herald* for copies of the articles Dobie used as sources. Those articles bore almost no similarity to the story Dobie recounted in *Apache Gold & Yaqui Silver*."[2]

One of the earlier covers for *Apache Gold & Yaqui Silver*.

As it turned out, Dobie could never find a coherent version of the Adams story. Or, that is to say, like the four gospels of the New Testament, there were differences in each telling of the tale. One old timer would claim the party consisted of over twenty men, while another might tally it at less than ten. Dates and locations were especially hard to pin down. Though Dobie set his tale in 1864, there were stories that placed the events either prior to 1864 or after. The location of the canyon, in particular, was hard to pin down, as it was never clear if the diggings were in Western New Mexico or Eastern Arizona, but Dobie settled on the Plains of San Agustin and the Datil Mountains of New Mexico for the most part.

In the old days, searches for the lost diggings put men in early graves, as evidenced by this account from the *El Paso Herald* of May 10, 1929, which spoke of all the men who had died or went insane from hunting the Adams Diggings. One of the more interesting portions of the article related,

> Old residents of the region from Silver City to Clifton, roughly bounding the area in which the "Adams Diggins" may have been, say that at least 15 persons to their knowledge have gone insane trying to find the "Diggins," and that 30 years ago a prospector shot and killed himself because he had sworn to find the fabulous lost placer claims or die in the attempt.[3]

The same *Herald* article noted that stories of the Lost Adams, which they had been publishing as early as 1921, "proved astonishingly popular." The article went on to state that every issue of that paper sold out "except those retained for our files" and that "the story was reprinted by request and the demand for reprints was extraordinary."

In the wake of the publication of *Apache Gold & Yaqui Silver,* the legend became even more popular and a new generation of Adams enthusiasts were born. Some seekers of the gold were amateurs, while others were professional prospectors. Though many claimed to have found the diggings over the years, no concrete proof ever emerged that anyone really did. What Dobie's book ensured more than anything was that the Adams legend would endure. From the 1930s on, nearly every book on southwestern treasure tales would include the Adams Diggings in some capacity. *Apache Gold & Yaqui Silver* also resulted in numerous articles in Western pulp magazines, each one adding their own variations to the legend, and it is from those dubious sources that this book takes its main inspiration.

So, once again, I'll reiterate that if you want to find the real diggings, you won't find them in the pages ahead, only the myth that they spawned. But, then again, where the Lost Adams is concerned, perhaps myth is the only truth.

Section Notes

---

[1] Simmons, *Treasure Trails of the Southwest*, p.93.

[2] Purcell, *Lost Adams Diggings*, Chapter 16.

[3] "15 MEN WENT INSANE HUNTING ADAMS DIGGINS SUICIDE ALSO AS PART OF THE FAMOUS GOLD LEGEND," *El Paso Herald* (May 10, 1929).

LOST ADAMS AT THE MOVIES

The Lost Adams story made it to the big screen via *Mackenna's Gold*, released in 1969. Though something of a Super-Western starring Gregory Peck and shot in Cinerama, it unfortunately flopped in the U.S. market. The film told of a return expedition to the Lost Adams Diggings and did not serve as an adaptation of the events put forth in J. Frank Dobie's *Apache Gold & Yaqui Silver*. Furthermore, being set in the 1880s, it didn't largely feature Adams himself, though he did appear in a short, supporting role well played by Edward G. Robinson. Meandering along somewhat aimlessly for over two hours (the original cut ran three), the film's ending, where the canyon is destroyed in an earthquake, at least gave the movie a grand sendoff. And while the idea of the canyon collapsing in an earthquake was similar to accounts related in *Black Range Tales* by James McKenna, *Mackenna's Gold* ironically bore no official relation to that book. Instead, it was based upon Will Henry's novel of the same name, which took inspiration from *Apache Gold & Yaqui Silver*.

1.

DOBIE'S GOLD

CREATING THE PASTICHE

As stated in the introduction, even more than Adams himself, it was probably J. Frank Dobie who propagated the myth of the diggings more successfully than anyone. And although others had told the tale before him, it was undoubtedly Dobie who firmly wedged it into the lore of the West for all time. As such, we will use his pastiche as the starting point for the basic Lost Adams Diggings story. If you know Dobie's version well, you might as well skip the next section, but following the Dobie version, all of the sources that inspired it and how they differed will be listed.

Apache Gold & Yaqui Silver In August of 1864, a man now known only as Adams had just delivered a load of freight to Tucson and was in the process of returning to his home in California.[1] While camped at the Gila Bend, he awoke to find a group of five Indians running off his horses, which were grazing some distance away from camp. Adams, who had been wise enough to tether at least one of his horses nearby, mounted it and gave chase, shooting down one of the Indians. When Adams returned to his camp, it had been ransacked. The five Indians were really just a distraction for others to raid his camp and take what they wanted.

Twenty miles to the north was a friendly village of Pima Indians, which Adams traveled to with what remained of his belongings. At the village, called Sacaton, he was elated to discover a group of twenty-one prospectors who offered to trade Adams for the dozen horses he had left. The men were excited over the story of a canyon of gold, told to them by a young Mexican man whom the Apache had captured in a raid and raised since he was a boy. Because of a deformed, knot-like ear, he was known as Gotch Ear. The young man had taken note of how excited the prospectors became over gold. Having been raised by the Apache, who cared little for the metal, he didn't realize gold could be traded for other goods. As such, he told the men of a hidden canyon in Apacheria, not more than ten days away. If they would give him two horses, a gun, and other provisions, he would be their guide to the canyon. If he failed to lead them there, he said that they could shoot him on the spot.

Hut made of arrowbrush and earth in Pima, Arizona, c. 1907. (Library of Congress, Edward S. Curtis.)

Though Adams had no interest in mining or prospecting, and this would be his first venture doing so, Adams was made leader of the party for some reason. The group left Sacaton on August 20, 1864, and counting Adams and the guide, there were twenty-three men total. They headed northeast in the direction of a landmark known as Mount Ord, and following that were two peaks, which Gotch Ear claimed the canyon was about six days from. Gotch Ear also noted that they were not far from the fort near the malpais, meaning Fort Wingate.

California 49ers on the trail of the Gold Rush.

Eventually the group came upon a bluff, and blending into it was a large boulder which served as a secret door into the canyon. The passageway was unique in the way that it literally zigzagged in the shape of a perfect gigantic Z. When the party entered the canyon, they found it to be something of an oasis of trees with a clear running stream and a waterfall. The men began panning the stream at once and found copious amounts of gold in no time. The prospectors erupted into jubilation as they held up their gold nuggets. Some panned from the river while others dug into the canyon walls to find a vein. It wasn't just the gold, but also the abundance of water, trees, grass, and animal life for hunting that made it the perfect spot. In short, it was a miner's dream come true, and even though Gotch Ear told the men that more gold could be found further away, the men decided to stay where they were. Perhaps their fate would have turned out differently had they followed Gotch Ear's advice to move onto the richer site.

Prospector panning for gold.

The first among the party to smell trouble was one simply called the Dutchman, who feared an Apache raid. As such, the Dutchman requested that he be able to work alone and leave the canyon on his own when he saw fit. Likewise, Gotch Ear promptly took his payment and left by nightfall of the first day. What later became of him is unknown.[2] As for Adams, as leader of the group, he was put in charge of all the gold, which was collectively stored so as to be split and divided equally at a later date. Nor did all the men pan for gold. Some were put to work building a cabin, which would go on to become a notable landmark in the Adams saga.

The next day mysteriously appeared a group of Apache led by Chief Nana. Oddly, Nana was not hostile towards the men and told them they were welcome to stay in what he called Sno-Ta-Hay Canyon so long as they didn't venture beyond the waterfall.[3] Adams assured Nana that they would honor his request, and he and his people went on their way. Ten days later, provisions began to run low, and it was decided six men should travel to Fort Wingate and purchase supplies. They divvied out gold to be used to buy ammunition, a whipsaw, and more mining equipment such as axes and pics. The man put in charge of this party, according to Dobie, was another notable survivor of the Adams saga, John Brewer, who would later recount his own version of the ordeal. When Brewer and his men departed, the Dutchman decided to go with them and leave the diggings for good.

Apache riders by Charles Craig.

While the six-man party proceeded on their voyage, which they estimated would take eight days, construction on the cabin continued with a fireplace and a large hearth, under which Adams hid much of the gold. As time stretched on, summer began to show the first signs of fall. Though the men still had more gold than they could ever wish for, they naturally still wanted more. Remembering what Nana said about not venturing above the falls, one of the men wondered if perhaps there was even more gold to be found there. There, he suspected, might even be the fabled mother lode. The man got his chance to explore the area when a couple of the party's horses wandered beyond the waterfall. While above the falls searching for the horses, the man found an especially large gold nugget. When he brought it back to camp, the other men couldn't resist sneaking above the waterfall themselves. As suspected, the area was even richer in gold.

Ominously, on the eighth day, the supply party failed to return as expected. Adams and another man named Davidson decided to ride out of the canyon to look for them. The decision would end up saving their lives. Outside of the secret door, they found the corpses of five men and several dead horses. Obviously, they had been slaughtered by the Apache. Adams and Davidson raced back through the zigzag trail, and by the time they returned to camp, a scene of violence unfurled before their horrified eyes. An Apache massacre was underway, with all of the miners being slaughtered one by one while the cabin burned to the ground.[4]

Geronimo and his warriors in Mexico c.1886.

Hiding amongst the rocks, Adams and Davidson laid away quietly while the Apache scoured the canyon for them. Eventually, they all rode away and under the cover of night

Adams and Davidson quietly crept back to camp, getting water from the stream and trying to secure as much gold as they could carry without horses.[5] Unfortunately for the two survivors, the hot smoldering remains of the cabin was too much for them to dig through. It pained the men to leave behind what they estimated to be more than $100,000 worth of gold hidden under the hearth. Nor could the men work to dig through the ashes to find it, for the noise might alert any Apache within earshot. All that Adams escaped with was a large nugget that had come from above the forbidden falls.

Traveling only at night, slowly the survivors made their way out of the canyon back to the secret door. Even once they escaped the canyon's confines, Adams and Davidson still only traveled at night for fear of the Apache discovering them. On the thirteenth day of their wanderings, they had the good fortune to be rescued by a cavalry from Fort Apache, Arizona.

Fort Apache c.1873.

While resting at Fort Apache, a commotion woke Adams from his sleep. Outside, he spotted five Apaches, whom he recognized from the canyon massacre. Either out of fear or vengeance, he took his gun and began firing on them, killing two Apache before he was disarmed by the soldiers. Because these Apache had come to the fort in peace, Adams was taken to the guardhouse to await trial for murder. Two nights later he escaped on a horse that he had stolen from a lieutenant. And from there, Adams made it back to Los Angeles where he stayed for several years.

According to Dobie, Adams didn't return to New Mexico until 1874 under the funding of a friend named Captain C.A. Shaw.[6] The expedition consisted of sixteen men and details are sparse where Dobie is concerned, but according to him, Adams "merely took a course that ended on the San Francisco River 100 miles north of where Silver City was soon to boom as a mining center."[7]

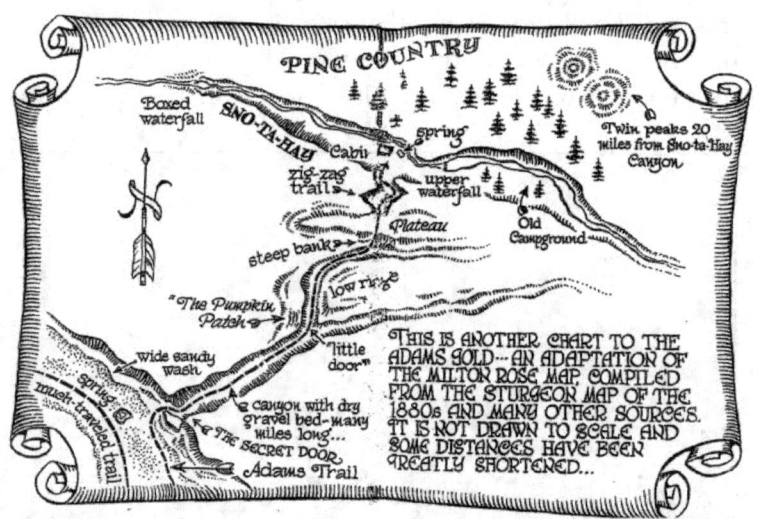

However, Shaw at least witnessed an exchange that added veracity to Adams' tale. While Shaw and Adams were together at the trading post at Fort Apache, Adams recognized Chief Nana.[8] Shaw observed Adams speak civilly with Nana for several minutes until Adams brought up Sno-Ta-Hay Canyon. After this, Nana glared at Adams for nearly a minute without speaking and then walked away.

Dobie said a third expedition occurred a few years later during the spring, with a little over twenty men following Adams out of San Bernardino, California, into northeastern Arizona. This time, when Adams failed to lead them to the gold, the "search ended in violent dissension," with the party accusing Adams of just using them "to get back into the gold country and then refusing to show what he recognized."[9]

The Silver Bar in Socorro, NM, c. the 1880s.
Did Adams ever tell his tale there?

Another expedition occurred in late 1880 into the winter of 1881 on behalf of a doctor who had treated Adams shortly after his 1864 ordeal. The source of this information was John F. Dowling, who reported that when he was in Socorro in January of 1881, he met a doctor named Sturgeon who was part of a "demoralized crowd of Adams Diggings hunters."[10] As it turned out, Sturgeon was none other than the post surgeon at Fort Apache when Adams and Davidson were brought there after thirteen days of wandering in the desert. According to Sturgeon,

> They were in a very serious condition both mentally and physically. I was called upon to care for them.... They told me, not very coherently, what they had been through. Adams showed me the solitary nugget of gold he had brought out and gave a description of the country. I wanted right then to organize an expedition and go back with Adams to the gold.[11]

25

The tale haunted Sturgeon's dreams for years until, in late 1880, he persuaded 40 other men, sometimes called "The Forty Thieves," to join him on an excursion into New Mexico. It was one of the more elaborate expeditions to find the Lost Adams as Dobie reported, "They had new rifles, new boots, collapsible water buckets, patented bedrolls, the finest equipment that Eastern supply houses could rig up."[12] The group traveled by railroad to Las Vegas, New Mexico, and then hired a wagon train to take them to Socorro. As it turned out, it was a very severe winter, and by January, most of the men with Sturgeon gave up.

In the 1880s, Adams was part of another well-equipped venture from California, which he brought to Milligan's Plaza. After two months and finding nothing, the men reportedly threatened to hang Adams. Just as he was about to be strung up, a friend named Washie Jones came along and rescued him and sent Adams back to Magdalena. Upon arriving there, Adams immediately took up residence in a saloon and got back to doing what he did best: telling his sad story. During this particular rendition, he berated the former commander of Fort Apache, stating how he refused to escort Adams back to the canyon to get the gold. As it turned out, a former sergeant. from Fort Apache was actually there in the bar. The sergeant then claimed that Adams was nothing but a horse thief who had actually stolen the gold. According to the sergeant, Adams and his compadres had either murdered the prospectors themselves, or had come upon the aftermath of an Apache massacre and taken the gold of the dead prospectors. Adams promptly fled the saloon when the sergeant threatened to kill him.

Adams sought the protection of a Magdalena-area lawman, Bob Lewis, soon after. During their time together, Adams admitted to Lewis that he had lied about the Fort Apache story. "The truth is there is one thing about the gold I have never told anybody and never will tell anybody," Adams told Lewis. "But there is gold all right. Go and look for the bones of those men who were carrying supplies into the canyon. Show me the bones, and I'll show you the gold."[13]

According to Dobie via Captain Shaw, Adams searched for the gold until it killed him. Adams was on one of his excursions into the mountains of New Mexico when he suffered a heart attack and was sent back home to California, where he died in 1886.

"The Lost Cabin Mine" *The Socorro Chieftain* was one of the earliest sources of the Adams tale that Dobie mined from. It was published in 1898 and came from W.W. Williams, who called it the "Lost Cabin Mine." It should be noted that Williams was a participant in one of the return expeditions comprising Adams and Captain Shaw. In his iteration, Adams' adventure occurred in the fall of 1858 with a party of twenty-two Californians who arrived at Yuma. (Williams was the first source to bump the party up to over twenty men and to replace Sacaton with Yuma as the Pima Indian village.)

The most interesting variation, though, was that the Apache attacked the men on the way to the canyon rather than after arriving there. During the attack, three men were killed, and the Apache were driven away. After this, the men marched onto the canyon unopposed, where they erected several cabins rather than just one. Furthermore, these cabins were constructed of stone rather than wood. The miners also collected nearly double the amount of gold in this iteration, estimated to be as high as $200,000's worth.

As usual, a detachment of men eventually left to go get supplies. In this case, instead of six days, six weeks passed without them returning. The Apache returned to attack the camp, causing Adams and his companion to run into the wilderness, nearly insane and starved by lack of food. Interestingly, in this version, Adams traveled to Brownsville, Texas, where he sailed back to California. Keeping in mind that this version of the story occurred in 1858, prior to the Civil War, Adams joined the California Column volunteers and returned to New Mexico during the war. There, he attempted to find his lost gold to no avail.

This rendition was given to Williams in 1883, and he reported that Adams returned to California soon after and died.[14]

GOLD

The Adams Gold Diggings

A TRUE STORY OF THE RICHEST GOLD
MINE IN ALL HISTORY

FOUND IN NEW MEXICO AND AGAIN
LOST

The Mines of Solomon, Klondike and the California don't compare in richness to these Adams Diggins'.

If you will read this story, it will tell, how YOU, may become a millionaire. Read it.

PRICE 50 CENTS.

By W. H. Byerts

The Adams Gold Diggings One of Dobie's favorite building blocks in concocting his version of the legend came from W.H. Byerts, who heard the story from Captain Shaw and published his pamphlet, *The Adams Gold Diggings*, in 1919.[15] Byerts' version didn't differ much from Dobie's. One glaring difference, though, was that Byerts oddly made Geronimo himself the Apache leader encountered at the canyon rather than Chief Nana.[16] Byerts also added a macabre flourish not seen in the other versions, that being that the Apache had beheaded some of the prospectors and stuck the severed heads on stakes. In the pamphlet, Byerts wrote, "Looking down we saw the heads of some of our companions extended high on polls, and the bucks and squaws were dancing around with the old familiar war whoop."

The John Brewer Account One of the more trustworthy accounts given on the Adams Diggings came from another survivor named John Brewer. His account was published in *The El Paso Herald* in 1928 by A.M. Tenney Jr. Brewer's version differed notably from Adams' and Shaw's. Firstly, he placed his adventure in the year 1862 rather than 1864. Brewer's party of prospectors was also much smaller, comprising only of himself and four other men as opposed to over twenty. Brewer and his four companions left California on a freight wagon bound for Arizona. There they met Brewer's version of Gotch Ear, who he described as a half-Pima and half-Mexican who, as usual, told them the tale of the gold canyon. After some palavering, Brewer and his four companions entered into an agreement with the Pima-Mexican guide for him to escort them to the canyon.

Adams entered the tale when he had a chance meeting with Brewer when the latter was scouring nearby ranches to procure horses for the expedition. Interestingly, Brewer never gave Adams a first name, nor was Adams identified as a fellow freighter. In Brewer's testimony, he was simply a mysterious man wandering the wilderness with a small remuda of horses. Though initially he agreed to rent the horses on reasonable terms, Adams later decided to join the expedition to share in the gold. In a sense, Brewer hired Adams as a trail boss with his horses, equipment, and everything else necessary for the party's expedition.

Brewer's story deviated significantly concerning the mining of the gold from the canyon. For instance, Brewer oddly said nothing of the construction of the cabin (though perhaps he

THE LOST BOOK OF ADAMS

The first book on the Adams Diggings was apparently compiled in the late 1890s but was destroyed before publication. Per Dobie in *Apache Gold & Yaqui Silver,* a silver magnate by the name of Colonel John B. Crawford had just gone belly up and decided to change hands to gold. As such, he compiled every existing piece of information on the Adams Diggings that he could find, resulting a 70,000-word manuscript. Oddly, he came to the conclusion that the diggings were in southwestern Utah of all places. Crawford prospected there with a party for five months. When he returned home, he destroyed his tome on the diggings. Either he found no gold and burned the book out of bitterness, or perhaps he did find gold and wanted to destroy any clues that might aid and abet others in finding it.

didn't think it important to the tale). Adams' exit from the story was also markedly different and had Adams and an unnamed companion set off in search of some missing horses, never to be seen again. In Brewer's version of the massacre, he reported how three of his companions, plus his version of Gotch Ear, set out to go panning for gold while Brewer stayed behind at the camp to do dishes. Dramatically, Brewer stated, "I heard a sound which I took to be distant thunder, but there was not a cloud to be seen." Brewer continued, "My next thought was that it was a mighty wind and as the sound increased and seemed to be drawing near a chill of wonder swept over me."

After this, Brewer observed his companions being massacred by what he estimated to be 100 Apache as opposed to Dobie's 300. Brewer remembered that "Suddenly they began to let forth horrifying screams and yells... and forming a cordon around the hopeless boys, butchered them in an instant." There being nothing that Brewer could do but watch, he naturally fled and recounted that, "The last horrifying glimpse I had of the massacre was of the reds apparently holding hands in a circle dancing around my dead companions and sending forth a bloodcurdling song."

As Brewer trekked across the desert, Tenney interestingly recorded Brewer calling out for Adams:

> As I turned to get out of sight I don't know what came over me but I caught myself streaking at the top of my voice, "Adams! Adams! My God, what shall I do!"[17]

After this, Brewer wandered the wilderness in a fashion befitting an Edgar Rice Burroughs yarn, being rescued on the sixth day by a tribe of Pueblo Indians who took him to a village along the Rio Grande. When he returned to civilization, Brewer worried about searching for Adams. Later in life, Brewer wondered, "Did I do right in escaping without waiting to find out what happened to Adams and the other men with him?" It was thought that Brewer escaped with enough gold to begin a ranch down in Mexico, where he lived comfortably for several years.

Among those who champion the John Brewer version today is author and prospector W.C. Jameson, who noted in his book *The Lost Canyon of Gold* the following:

> Brewer's version smacks of the unvarnished rendering of an experience. He told of finding gold, harvesting it, and then fleeing as a result of the Indian menace. There were no heroics, no dramatic or mythological elements of a quest replete with obstacles and threshold guardians. Dobie's telling of the story of the lost canyon of gold, on the other hand, is full of adventure and a number of elements that appear almost too good to be true.[18]

The Adams Diggings Story Aside from early-day newspaper reports, one of the first more widely published versions of the tale was *The Adams Diggings Story* by Charles Allen, published in 1935. And though Allen never met Adams, he did meet his chief disciple, Captain Shaw. As this was one of Dobie's primary sources, Allen's account was naturally quite similar to *Apache Gold & Yaqui Silver* aside from a few minor details Dobie felt didn't fit his narrative. One of the problems facing

Dobie as he cobbled together Adam's route were the numerous differences in locations, and perhaps it's no surprise that Allen and Dobie differed in this particular regard.

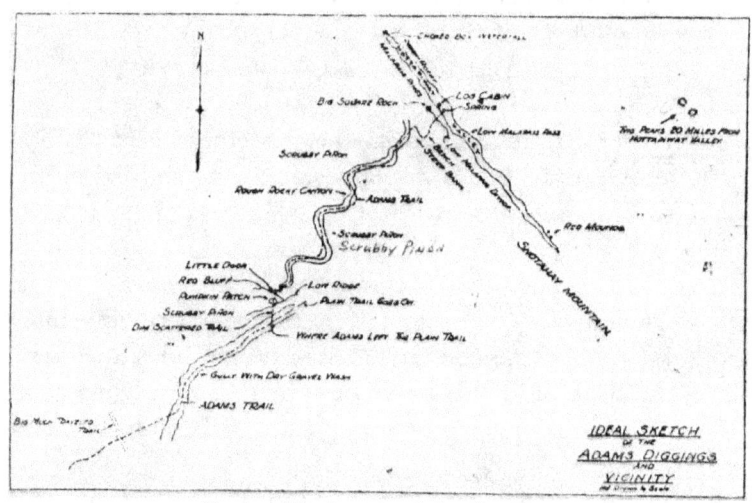

Charles Allen's map of the diggings.

Oddly, whereas Dobie used the name Sno-Ta-Hay Canyon, Allen spoke of a Sno-Ta-Hay Mountain and called the canyon Hot-ta-pi-wat for reasons unknown. Nor was Gotch Ear named in Allen's rendition, though he served the same role. In Allen's version, the Mexican guide also told the miners that some peaks in the distance provided "coarser and more plentiful" gold. "As Adams never went east of Hot-ta-pi-wat valley, and it did not climb its northeast side, he knew nothing about the two peaks country or the placers near them," Allen recorded.

Rather than it taking eight days for Adams to begin worrying about the supply party, after six days, Adams became concerned and set out on the seventh day with Davidson to look for them. Together, Adams and Davidson found nine of the men outside of the canyon and returned to find their friends in the process of being slaughtered. Allen's only other real notable alteration was that rather than selling his gold nugget in Tucson for $92 as per Dobie, Allen said Adams sold his nugget in Los Angeles for $93.

Allen also provided more details on the Dutchman, claiming that he traveled to Yuma, Arizona, and sold his gold to a storekeeper there named Hinton. As such, in Yuma the lost canyon was known as the Dutchman's Diggings. With the money from the gold, the unnamed German started a cattle ranch near Prescott, where Allen said he was killed by Apaches in 1867.[19]

Allen also offered some interesting variations on the elderly Davidson, who was often reported to have died not long after the incident. Contrary to this, Allen noted that while Captain Shaw and Adams were in New Mexico on a return trip to look for the diggings,

> Adams received a letter from his wife in Los Angeles stating that Jack Davidson was in town, had called on her, and that he was much disappointed; said the principal reason for his journey from Fort Whipple was to meet Adams. They never met. Davidson died. He was a much older man than Adams.

Dobie probably felt it more dramatic to let Davidson die shortly after the event, though in Dobie's defense, the death of Davidson was the norm in most accounts.

Chapter Notes

[1] In addition to August 1864, other proposed dates for the expedition ranged all the way back to 1850 and up to 1866.

[2] Dobie added that two of Nana's men were later seen riding the horses belonging to Gotch Ear, so it's implied that the Apache killed him.

[3] There were alternating reasons as to why the waterfall was a no-no, though in Dobie's version he said it was because the Apache were camping there for a time.

[4] Dobie's version of the canyon certainly must have been sizable, for he claimed that there were no less than 300 Indians at work scalping and mutilating the bodies of the dead miners.

[5] Adams' and Davidson's horses wandered off long ago, while the Apache absconded with the rest.

[6] Shaw was important because he received the story of the diggings directly from Adams himself.

[7] Dobie, *Apache Gold & Yaqui Silver*, p.30.

[8] This added up with historical accounts which stated that Nana's Apaches were moved to San Carlos in 1874 from Fort Apache.

[9] Dobie, *Apache Gold & Yaqui Silver*, pp.31-32.

[10] Ibid, p.35.

[11] Ibid, pp.35-36.

[12] Ibid, p.36.

[13] Ibid, p.43.

[14] This more or less matched up with the date of Adams' death in 1886.

[15] Full title: *The Adams Gold Diggings: A True Story of the Richest Gold Mine In All History*.

[16] Another account made Cochise the Apache chief in the story.

[17] I found this bit interesting and halfway wondered if it was an addition made by Tenney. I say this because it gave it a rather dramatic flair and I had to wonder if it was added only after Adams became so heavily associated with the legend. It was also a little suspicious because Brewer never named any of the other men in his party except for Adams, who was quite well-known by the publication of this article.

[18] Jameson, *Lost Canyon of Gold*, p.51.

[19] Jack Purcell and others discovered the name of the Dutchman: Jacob Snively. Purcell found that rather than Yuma, Arizona, it was at Pinos Altos, New Mexico, where the Dutchman arrived with a mule loaded with $10,000 worth of gold. Perhaps to protect himself and the location of the gold, Snively never told a story similar to that of the Adams Diggings of a party of white prospectors massacred by Apache. As such, his gold was known as the Lost Snively Diggings. And indeed, Snively was killed by the Apache at Vulture Gluch, Arizona, in March of 1871 rather than 1867.

2.

APOCRYPHA OF ADAMS
LESSER-KNOWN VERSIONS OF THE MYTH

If that first chapter was a bit of a drag for you as a necessary rehash of the legend, then this section should be where you can find a few new nuggets, though I suspect they are mostly fool's gold. The *Syracuse Standard* of March 7, 1897, summed it up pretty well when they said, "Now, when a New Mexico prospector is hard up he tells the story of the Lost Adams to some confiding persons, gets a grubstake and disappears." Or, in other words, if a man wanted to go prospecting and had no money, he might pretend to be Adams in an effort to get financing. Needless to say, those scenarios usually didn't end well for either party. These tales from Adams' pretenders also resulted in a deluge of disinformation. It's no wonder why Howard Bryan, the beloved columnist who wrote "Off the Beaten Path," once mused, "The more I learn about the lost Adams diggings, the more confused I get about the whole thing."[1]

E.V. Batchler of Catron County, New Mexico, gave a good account of what could be called the legend of the legend in a 1938 Federal Writer's Project interview entitled "The Adams Diggings":

> Since I came to New Mexico 18 years ago, I have heard stories of the wealth of the famous, old lost Adams Diggings Mine. I have heard at least a dozen different

stories and each succeeding story made the mine richer both in actual gold value and romantic interest. As is often the way of lost mines of this type, it all depends on who you listen to, whether the mine gets richer or not. It always seemed strange to me that nearly every old-timer will swear that he knows more about a fabulously rich, lost mine than any other old prospector. He will try to discredit other prospectors who have searched for the mine and in an effort to tell something "bigger" will magnify its riches by manyfold what others have estimated it at. In reality, none of them know or have the slightest idea as to the value of the lost mine, because it has never been found.

Even the *El Paso Herald*'s semi-classic 1927 piece, "Following the Will o' Wisp, 'The Lost Adams Diggin's'," admitted that there were by then "infinite variations of the tale."[2] It is the differences in these "infinite variations" that will be discussed next.

"A LOST GOLD MINE" As published in the *Boston Sunday Post* of September 19, 1897, this accounting of Adams came from a former soldier from the Sixth Calvary, Ed. E. Gosse, under the command of a Captain Madden. In 1885 the cavalry was in the Mogollon Mountains when they came upon the remains of a dead prospector who had apparently been killed by the Apache. Within his pockets were letters from a party in Silver City who claimed that they had found the "mother lode." Another letter on the man seemed to imply that he had himself discovered the diggings. This piqued an interest in the diggings among the soldiers. When they arrived in Duncan, Arizona, Gosse visited with the village blacksmith and asked his opinion of the Adams story. To his surprise, the blacksmith informed him that he was one of the original California 49ers and that he had known Adams personally. Not only that; he claimed he had seen the gold that Adams had brought back with him. In his own words, "I know it sounds like a romance, but I had it straight from Adams himself – not secondhand, like some of the stories you hear of it."

View of the Mogollon Range c.1939 as seen from Highway 260.
(W. H. Shaffer, FS #383788)

What follows are the relevant portions of the article relating to this iteration of the Adams story:

THE OLD BLACKSMITH'S STORY

To begin with, old man Adams had always got along with the Indians in a very friendly way, somehow or other. Whether he sold them ammunition or not I don't know, but nevertheless they never molested him. He noticed that some of them had ornaments made out of pure gold – hammered out with stones. Some had just the nuggets tied to a buckskin string. All his efforts to induce them to tell where they got this gold failed, until at last he bribed an Indian boy by the promise of a lot of ponies to show him the place.

At last Adams and the two partners, with the boy, started in. They had a couple of burros loaded with their outfit, and traveled, as Adams told me, in parallel lines so as to leave as little of a trail as possible. They located the place, put up a "shack" and went to work. They had plenty of water in a creek close by, which Adams always said had a peculiar color. Never before had they struck

37

anything so rich as these diggings. As fast as they washed the gold out they buried it, from fear of being surprised by the Indians. Well, their "grub" began to run short, and they drew lots to see which one would go out with the boy for a fresh supply. It fell to the lot of Johnson (Clark and Johnson were the names of the two men who went with Adams), and he started back with the boy for the provisions. After waiting a reasonable time for them to get back, and their "grub" getting lower and lower every day, and still no signs of them, old Adams declared he would go back and see if he could find them, thinking they might have got lost in the mountains. After going back on the trail a couple of days he found the bodies of Johnson and the boy. They had been killed by the Indians.

Old man Adams was staggered. He knew then the Indians were on their trail. He turned back to the diggings, traveling night and day, to notify his other partner. When he got there he found the Indians had been there before him and had killed Clark.

The old man dug up as much of the gold they had buried as he dared to carry, and grabbing a piece of 'sow-belly' and a chunk of bread, he started by a circuitous route for the nearest settlement.

Thus ended the relevant portion of the article. It was suspect not only in how it varied from the usual version, but also because the Apache did not care for gold ornaments. Not only that, the story had some similarities to the account of "Adams Cave," a separate treasure involving a different man named Adams. In that case, Henry Adams was an Indian trader at Fort Defiance, Arizona, who noticed the Navajo often carried gold with them into his store. Perhaps the old blacksmith heard both tales and conflated them on accident. As it stands, Adams being friendly with the Indians better matched that of Henry Adams who ran the trading post at Fort Defiance. Whether the old blacksmith was just confusing his stories, or telling a tall tale on purpose, this one is certainly just fool's gold.

The Wilbur B. Cassady Account Howard Bryan was easily one of the greatest compilers of Lost Adams tales, second only, perhaps, to Dobie. One of the accounts that Bryan unearthed was that of Wilbur B. Cassady, a pioneer of Socorro. Cassady wrote a letter to Bryan claiming that the Lost Adams Diggings were actually the remains of an old Spanish gold mine. Stranger yet, Cassady claimed that the story's namesake, Adams himself, was among the prospectors who died during the Apache massacre.

In the spring of 1928, none other than Western novelist Zane Grey came to Cassady's ranch. Along with Gray was Captain Shaw (now in his nineties), two men from the Smithsonian, and another writer by the name of Thomas. The men wanted to meet the grandfather of Cassady's wife, who was an old stagecoach driver from Socorro by the name of "Blanco" Jim Taylor. Somehow, Shaw knew that two of the survivors of the Apache massacre, again not Adams in this case as he was dead, had come by Taylor's ranch many years ago. Cassady arranged the meeting as desired and took them to see Taylor, who confirmed that a mysterious man had come to his ranch some years ago. The man took a meal and bought some supplies with a large gold nugget. (Interestingly, Taylor had the nugget forged into a watch charm.) Later, another man who was wounded came onto the ranch. Taylor took him to a doctor in Socorro, but the man died. Before expiring, the man told Taylor and others that he and one other man had escaped an Indian attack while they were working an old mine. The entrances to the mine, he claimed, "were on a second rise above an arroyo and faced the east. The second entrance was about 100 yards back on the north side. On the first rise they had built cabins, and it was there that the Indians first attacked."[3]

Did Zane Grey really team up with Captain Shaw to go on a hunt for the Lost Adams? And if so, was Grey more concerned with finding actual gold or simply in gathering stories for a potential Western novel? In any case, this was the only tie I found linking Grey to the Lost Adams.

Zane Grey c.1925.

The Rodgers Rendition On February 2, 1912, the *Sierra County Advocate* published a very interesting letter from Mr. Clark Rodgers of Lone Mountain, Grant County, New Mexico, to the *Silver City Enterprise*. The subject of the letter, of course, was the Lost Adams, and Rodgers' version had a few interesting details and alterations. Adams was given the initials of A.V. Adams, though other than naming him, he had no real role in Rodgers' rendition. Interestingly, though, Rodgers' account alluded to the possibility that Adams and his party were soldiers, a theory put forth by credible researchers like Jack Purcell. Rodgers' source for the Adams story was the son of a heretofore unknown member of the party with the surname of Forsythe, a soldier who had been honorably discharged from "Fort Franklin" in El Paso in the 1850s. Rodgers implied that this excursion occurred prior to 1864, possibly right after Forsythe's discharge. Rodgers wrote:

Presumably, "Fort Franklin" was Fort Bliss, pictured above c.1885.

There was a party of eight men, including Mr. Forsythe's father, who were talking of going to California. A half-breed Indian or Mexican who overheard them talking said, "I can show you where there is plenty of gold nearer than California." They listened to his tale, and becoming convinced of his truthfulness, they went with him, crossing the Rio Grande somewhere in the vicinity of Socorro. Then they turned west and in seven or eight days came to the diggin's and found the Indian's tale was true as there was plenty of gold. They killed elk and deer and had plenty of meat, but the guide told them not to shoot any oftener than necessary as there were many hostile Indians in the country. On the seventh day there was a band of half-naked Indians jumped them and told them to leave the country at once. This they lost no time in doing. In escaping they lost a boy 16 or 17 years old. He either fell asleep or the Indians captured him. Any way they did not know whatever became of him. Sergeant Forsythe told me his father brought home gold he gathered in this wild region...

A bit later, Rodgers also mentioned Forsythe passing away in California, which recalled the death of Davidson in California. As usual, Rodgers presented what was basically the same story but with altered names and dates.

The Dud Elridge Account The *El Paso Herald* of May 10, 1929, printed the testimony of Dud Elridge, a "pioneer cattleman of Greenlee county," who arrived in Clifton, Arizona, in 1887. There, he immediately heard the tale of the Adams diggings, which he claimed occurred in 1875 and comprised of Adams, an unnamed partner, and eight other men sans any Indian guides. In this version, Adams and the unnamed partner stayed behind to pan for gold while the other eight men left to go get supplies. Curiously, it was implied that the Apache attacked Adams and his friend and that, miraculously, Adams got away only wounded while the friend was killed.

Elridge's account stated,

> In the attack Adams was wounded and his partner killed. After hiding out a few days, Adams wandered south for many days, finally arriving on the outskirts of the old pueblo, where he was assisted into town, later going to California to recuperate.

The reference to the "old pueblo" clearly indicated this was actually the story of John Brewer, who recuperated at a pueblo along the Rio Grande. According to the article, "Adams was hazy about it all from his severe scalp wounds," thus implying that the Apache had attempted to scalp him.

The Herald article went on to admit that Elridge's story differed "in several unimportant particulars from the 'Adams Diggins' stories" that the paper had published in the past. It surmised, "The Elridge story herewith is a very condensed, almost bald narrative of a yarn which required columns to tell in all its glamorous and thrilling detail." Intriguingly the paper also added, "Somewhere in our desk is a hitherto unpublished 'Adams Diggins' story which will be dug out one of these days and given the light of day."

"The Adams Diggings" by E.V. Batchler During the 1930s, the Federal Writer's Project set out to interview the many "old-timers" who had survived the Old West. Many tall tales sprang from these FWP reports, among them a few on the Lost Adams. E.V. Batchler of Catron County was interviewed in 1938. He began his rendition of the diggings by berating the countless old timers who had exaggerated the tale. Then, Batchler proceeded with his own account, based upon what he had collectively gleaned over his past eighteen years in New Mexico. His version had Adams and his companions, sans Gotch Ear or any equivalent, setting out from Magdalena on their way back to California.

They stumbled across the gold purely by accident when seeking a stream for water. Within it, they spotted gold flecks. Batchler related, "Adams, who knew a little more about mining than his companions, decided the gold was shed into the stream from a rich outcropping above the camp." Adams then took "his partner," Davidson, and "traveled up the canyon about a mile to try to discover the 'mother lode'." And indeed, the two found an outcropping of quartz they believed to be the source of the gold in the stream.

While off exploring, Adams and Davidson heard gunshots and other sounds of violence. Rather than racing back to camp, the duo hid until they were sure it was safe to come out. It was unclear if Adams and Davidson witnessed the massacre or not, and oddly this rendition included no warning from Chief Nana and his Apache. Instead, the Apache showed up to massacre the miners without any foreshadowing. In any case, after Adams and Davidson were sure it was safe, they surveyed the damage and buried the dead.

Adams and Davidson then traveled to Fort Union, where they were denied aid to return to the canyon. The two then went to Reserve, New Mexico, showing off the ore samples they procured, and from there went to Pima, Arizona. There, Adams had friends who he thought might mount an expedition. Whereas usually it took Adams at least ten years to return to the area of the diggings, in this version he and his investors did so at once, though to no avail as usual.

Cow Dust and Saddle Leather Another variation of the Adams legend was recounted in *Cow Dust and Saddle Leather* by Ben Kemp and J.C. Dykes. The authors got their version from Washie Jones, an old timer who heard the tale directly from Adams in the year 1892. Of course, there were those who said that Adams died a few years before that, and as such, some wondered if Jones had his dates wrong and perhaps heard it in the 1880s. In any case, his version contained interesting variations. Notably, Jones placed the action on either a Navajo or a Zuni reservation in 1865. Interestingly, the Gotch Ear-type guide was a Mexican Indian scout for the Army, the only account where he served this role. Another troublesome variation was that Fort Apache replaced Fort Wingate, problematic because Fort Apache was established five years after this story's 1865 setting. Comprised of only five men, not including Adams and the guide, this tale also offered one of the smallest iterations of the Adams party. Instead of finding gold upon immediately entering the canyon, it was discovered as one of the men dug a hole for water.

Soon after, the guide left and Adams supposed that he had been killed before he could get back to Fort Apache. The most unique alteration was that this was the only version where the Dutchman served as the lone survivor with Adams. As usual, a party had gone to get supplies, leaving only Adams and the Dutchman behind. Five days passed without their return, and Adams and the Dutchman set out to find them on the sixth day. Perched atop a high ridge on the side of the canyon, they spotted the remains of the party, obviously massacred by the Apache.

After this, Adams and the Dutchman returned to the canyon to find their cabin on fire courtesy of the Apache. Adams and the Dutchman fled into the wilderness and, in this case, were found by soldiers from Fort Wingate traveling to Fort Tularosa. There, "Adams and the Dutchman were so weak from starvation and exposure they were out of their minds and unable to talk."[4] Interestingly, Adams led the soldiers back to the scene of the massacre outside of the canyon. As such, the dead men were given a proper burial though Adams and the Dutchman are too frightened to even attempt to reenter the canyon and vowed to do so only after the country had become "more civilized."[5]

The experience continued to plague Adams upon returning to California, where he contracted a severe attack of typhoid fever which nearly killed him. This incident caused him to lose his memory for a time, which is why he was unable to find the return route to the canyon when he came back to New Mexico and Arizona years later, or so this version claimed.

"I Found the Lost Adams Diggings" This account, published in the July 1945 issue of *New Mexico Magazine*, was written by Victoria Gray, wife of Captain James B. Gray, who served with the Roughriders during the Spanish American War and later served as chief of scouts for the Chiricahua Apache Reservation. Gray was among those who claimed to have rediscovered the diggings. In relating his story, he naturally gave his own unique account of the original Adams party, which he got from a man named Cooley, who had heard the tale straight from Adams.[6]

San Xavier Mission in Tucson.

In Cooley's version, rather than Sacaton, it was the San Xavier mission near Tucson, Arizona, where Adams met Gotch Ear in the year 1864. This party consisted of eleven men, including the guide along with twenty burros, which accounted for the slow nature of the journey. In addition to the group consisting of eleven men, the journey took eleven days. (This iteration of the tale also included the landmark of a mountain resembling a woman as did a few others.)

The miners worked the canyon for two days before deciding that they needed to return to Tucson for supplies. Nine of the men left, leaving Adams and Davidson alone in the canyon, their job being to construct a cabin in their absence. The men were gone for twenty-three days as Adams and Davidson continued to mine for gold while also building the cabin. Notably, in this iteration, there was no meeting with Chief Nana or any other Apache. Instead, on the twenty-second day, Adams and Davidson began to hear yelling and shooting off in the distance. The two men exited the canyon to investigate and found all of their companions dead, obviously massacred by Indians. Captain Gray also greatly exaggerated the amount of gold Adams escaped with, claiming that he was able to sell it for $22,000.

Navajo Gold The *Phoenix Arizona Republican* of January 2, 1902, included another unique alteration to the story, setting it on a Navajo reservation:

> A dozen or more years ago, an American named Adams came hurrying from the Navajo country into the coal mining town of Gallup, on the Santa Fe Pacific road, in western New Mexico, literally weighed down with huge nuggets of pure gold.
>
> The people in the locality at once became wild with excitement. Adams told how he, with several comp-anions, had discovered a rich mine in the Navajo reservation, and how they were just gathering from the surface such huge nuggets as he carried with him, when they were all raided by a hostile band of the Indians. While fleeing for their lives all were butchered excepting himself.
>
> A large party was at once organized with sufficient strength to recover the mine, but Adams, who held the key to the situation, succumbing to the excitement of his

terrible ordeal and narrow escape meanwhile went raving mad and had to be confined in an insane asylum, in which he soon afterward died. The party, however, attempted the recovery of the gold, but soon returned unsuccessful.

With the aid of the Navajos themselves this party came upon gold in the Carriso [sic] mountains, in the northern part of the reservation, and this was believed to be the lost Adams mine. But the gold in sight occurred only in small quantities, and it was decided that it would not pay to mine it. In and about Gallup there are still many men, witnesses of the arrival of Adams, among whom there is serious doubt as to whether that found by the army expedition is the mine which, before the collapse of his mind, he described in such glowing terms.[7]

B.D. Nichols Account *The El Paso Herald* of July 2, 1927, gave the account of B.D. Nichols, an El Paso mining man who claimed to have met Adams in the year 1883 at Warners Ranch, later was known as Hot Springs, in California. Nichols had already heard the tale of the Adams diggings before and wanted to hear it from the source himself. Adams told Nichols that in the early 1860s, when he was in California, he owned a ranch north of Hot Springs with "lots of cattle and green," but that he lacked "ready money." Adams continued that he heard that the freighting business was lucrative in Arizona, so in 1862 he equipped himself with an eight-horse team and set out for Tucson.

Afterward, Adams met five men plus the Mexican guide. Instead of Adams accompanying them to the gold immediately, the deal fell through in this version and Adams left them to head back to California. After leaving Tucson and camping at Picket Post, Adams' horses wandered away in the night and appeared to have taken the trail back to Tucson. Adams found them about five miles away and when he returned, he discovered renegade Indians destroying his camp. According to Nichols, Adams saw about forty braves dancing around his wagons as they burned.

John LeMay

Postcard depicting Picket Post, where Adams camped in this iteration.

Down on his luck, Adams returned to Tucson, where he reconnected with the miners and decided he didn't have anything to lose and might as well try his hand at finding the gold with them. In this version, the small group traveled for five and a half days until, on the sixth, they came upon a mesa with a canyon running through it. This rendition included the Dutchman, who accompanied Adams to round up some stray horses, which is how they survived the Apache raid that followed. In this version, Adams apparently blocked out his desert wandering because the last thing that he remembered was watching the Apache massacre before he woke up in the guardhouse of Fort West, twenty-five miles west of Silver City. "He was told that a scouting party had picked him up about four or five days travel to the northwest, naked and stark crazy," Nichols recounted.

After this, the story concluded as usual, with Adams killing some Apache at the fort, becoming a fugitive, and returning to California. In Nichols' opinion,

In those days following his escape from the Indians and before the soldiers found him, the idea of the mine was born in his tortured mind. Probably the party did find some gold, but it wasn't nearly as rich a deposit as Adams thought after he went mad from hunger, thirst and exhaustion.

Illustration of Tucson c. 1862.

ADAMS PLACERS AGAIN TO FRONT A hunt for the diggings by the "Lowell party" in 1906 resulted in yet another very different version of the legend being reprinted in the *Bisbee Daily Review* of August 17, 1906. It set the story in the 1850s, ten years prior to the usual date:

In the year of 1853 a party of twenty-four, headed by Adams, left overland from Missouri for the wilds of California. They were a hardy lot and used to the rugged deprivations of the west and accepted the hazardous task with no forebodings of the future. After a trying journey of several months they reached the wild White Mountains that separate Arizona from New Mexico.

At or near the highest peak of the range of mountains the famous Adams placers were found. The ground was literally covered with golden nuggets, and the Adams party collected as many as they could. Legend has it that some of the nuggets were as large as a man's thumb, and of pure gold. The party not wishing to give up the field, it was decided among them that twelve would proceed to San Francisco to dispose of what gold they could carry, and return to the new camp with money and provisions.

The twelve never reached their destination. They encountered a roving band of White Mountain Apaches

49

and were massacred to a man. Shortly afterwards the men left in the camp shared the same fate, the Indians learning that their diggings had been discovered. Adams was the only man to reach civilization alive, after untold hardships.

He went to California and remained in San Francisco and the mining counties of the North for a long time, returning to Arizona in the early 60's. He made a diligent search for his placers, but was never able to find them, although it was said that in early days Adams made a shipment of gold nuggets from Tombstone. Where they were found he never stated.

There is living today at Fort Apache, in Northern Arizona, an old Indian chief who once related how the white men were killed, when they started on their trip for San Francisco. It is said they fought like demons, and not until they had killed double their number of Indians were they exterminated. They were probably the first white party that had ever visited that portion, and the Apaches did not know how to handle them.

Adams lived many years following in Arizona, and passed through the vicissitudes of the old-time Arizonan. Three or four years ago he died in Los Angeles, the papers of that city giving quite an extended account of his life and of the famous Adams diggings.

Before he died, however, he made a map of the location of his placers and turned it over to some friends. He said that the diggings were located at the foot of a high peak in the White Mountains, from which point four rivers found their sources. It is supposed that this peak is Mt. Thomas. The placer was reached by going up a precipitous river bed between two frowning walls of granite, and otherwise described the place as one difficult of access. Scores of prospectors have tried to follow the directions but nothing has ever came of them.

"THE ADAMS DIGGINGS: The Interesting Story of the Mythical Lost Mine" A letter by George R. Spooner was published in the *Albuquerque Democrat* and reprinted in the

Arizona Republican on March 11, 1898. Spooner's account was another that placed the events prior to 1864, and had Adams keeping his gold nugget for 25 years rather than cashing it in.

In the fall of the year 1850 while the gold fever of California was at its height, a man by the name of Adams and his three companions were crossing New Mexico on their way to California. Late one evening they came to a path which led them up a short canyon to where they found water and it may be remarked here that water is scarce in that part of the country. They struck camp for the night and during the evening one of the men concluded to try a pan of dirt, and to his great surprise found gold in great abundance. After they were satisfied that they had struck it rich they went to work and built a miners' cabin and prepared to pass the winter in working their claim. In building the fireplace to the cabin they made a box of stone with the hearth rock as a covering for a place of safety to store their earnings. When they had been working the mine for about three months Adams took his gun one evening and went out to kill a deer for meat. When he returned late in the evening he found one of his partners lying in the trail about 100 yards from the cabin, where he had been killed by the Indians. On closer investigation he found the other two killed and the cabin burned down. The first thought with Adams was to get away from there as far and as fast as possible, and as California had been their objective point he started in that direction. As there was no living in that country and the Indians were always on the warpath in that day and time, he traveled in the night and lay by in the day time. After two nights' travel and about 9 o'clock a.m. on the third day he came to a stream of water at which point he marked a cottonwood tree so that he might have something as a guide to assist him in locating his mines sometime in the near future. He then made his way in a westerly direction, traveling for days and days, or rather nights, without seeing anyone until at last he landed in California. He there was engaged in different occupations for about twenty-five years, but at all times with the intention of closing out his business and returning to his rich mine in southern New Mexico whenever the country was sufficiently settled to make it safe for him to return. In about the year '78 Mr. Adams sold his two farms in California, which brought him $14,000. He then returned to New Mexico and began a systematic search for the mine.

On his return to the country where he thought he might be getting somewhere in the vicinity of his lost mine he found a few mining towns scattered over the country. He informed some of the best men of the country as to his business there, which created quite an excitement. He told them of how he had marked the cottonwood tree; he also produced a nugget of gold that he had taken from the mine and had carefully kept for twenty-five years. He described the stream upon whose banks the marked tree was growing. Some of the old timers who had heard and become interested in his story concluded to help him look for the marked tree, thinking if they found it as described there must be something in the story. After a diligent search of a few days the stream was located. It is now known as the Negrito, or Little Black. It is a tributary of the Gila and heads up in the Datil mountains. After a further search of a day or two the tree was found and was marked just as described by Adams, and showed to have been marked many years. Those who were present when the marked tree was found say that old man Adams was wild with joy and said, "Now, if the mine can be found I will be a millionaire and I only want what is hid under the hearth stone, and there are millions in the mines for others."

Adams and his party began searching for the mine proper. They thought the mine would be some forty or fifty miles from the marked tree, so they began the search on that theory, supposing that Adams would have traveled about twenty or twenty-five miles in a night. Adams continued the search for about twelve or fourteen years and squandered the whole of his $14,000 long before he gave up the search; in fact, he never quit hunting for that mine until death claimed him as its own. He died a poor, old broken hearted man, always saying that there were millions in the mine if it could be found.

"BURIED TREASURE: A Lost Gold Mine" This one seemed to be another variation of the "Lost Cabin Mine" version first printed in the late 1890s. It came from the *Manchester Evening News* of October 31, 1904, out of Britain under the header of "BURIED TREASURE: A Lost Gold Mine."

The mystery of the Adams Diggings seems to deepen as the years go by. A fabulously rich mine was discovered and lost in 1859 on the boundary of New Mexico and Arizona.

Twenty-two men in 1858 penetrated the then unknown desert to the south-west of California. At Yuma, on the Rocky Mountain ridge, they met a Mexican, who piloted the party up the Gila River for a distance of over 300 miles. When the point was reached where three mountain peaks stood out in the form of a triangle a halt was called. A camp was made, and the next day the prospectors discovered lumps of pure gold at the base of the nearest peak.

Six weeks' work enabled the party to accumulate an amount of gold estimated in value at £50,000. As supplies were running low, and tools for the work were badly needed, it was resolved that twelve of their number should take the gold to San Francisco.

Lots were drawn, and the twelve men selected set out with their golden burden. Twelve miles away they were murdered to a man by Apache Indians. Two days later all but one of those left behind at the camp were also butchered by the savages.

The man to escape was one named Adams, and, after terrible privations, he reached Fort Bliss laden with nuggets. The Civil War breaking out prevented an expedition setting out in search of the placer mountain for many years, but in 1883 Adams led a party up the Gila River, but so altered had the landmarks become that he failed to locate the mine.

Since then thousands of men have searched for the treasure, large sums of money have been spent, and many lives have been lost in the quest. Today, after forty-five years of fruitless search, the interest taken in the recovery of the mine is greater than ever, and less than a month ago an expedition of twenty-four men, consisting of mining experts, engineers, and geographical students started to wrest the secret from the vast rugged region bearing Adams' name.

Acoma Pueblo, which pilot Jerry Phillips spied from the air while searching for the Adams Diggings.

"A Pilot's Perspective on the Lost Adams" The fall 1975 issue of *Gold!* magazine contained a fascinating article by pilot Jerry Phillips on how he was hired to do an aerial search for the Lost Adams. Phillips was recruited by a man identified only as Baker, who had teamed with two brothers with the last name of Villareal. As usual, they had their own slant on the Adams diggings, which Baker told Phillips were discovered "immediately after the Civil War."

[Baker] told how [the Adams party] finally found free gold and untold quantities in a volcanic canyon at the base of an elusive landmark known as Twin Peaks and how Indians had swooped down at night and massacred all but two before they could transport their wealth out of the wilderness. Adams had been one of the survivors; and with a flour sack of nuggets had made his way out of the malpais, south and east. Traveling by night and hiding during the day he reached civilization and finally arrived in El Paso. After cashing in his nuggets for more than $3,000 he confided in a friend and left a written record of his experience.[8]

Postcard of Magdalena c.1919, when Johnston was growing up.

Old Magdalena Cow Town Magdalena old-timer Langford Johnston published his memoirs, *Old Magdalena Cow Town*, in 1983, and, for the author, the Adams Diggings were a way of life. "Every time my father went to Magdalena two or three people would talk to him about the Adams Diggings and want to go with him to look for it," he related in his chapter on the diggings.[9]

Johnston's rendition of the Adams tale was fairly close to Dobie's and came from Captain Shaw firsthand to Johnston's father. Johnston placed the events in the summer of 1864 and had Adams taking the same familiar route from Tucson to the

Gila Bend. Oddly, rather than traveling to a friendly Pima village in this version, Adams believed it was the usually friendly Pimas that ran off his horses, ransacked his camp, and lit his wagon on fire. After recouping his remuda, Adams went to Maricopa Wells, about 30 miles away, to see a friend.

Illustration of wagon train at Maricopa Wells in 1857.

As Adams' money had burned up in his wagon, he was so despondent that he sought refuge in a saloon even though he rarely "took more than two drinks."[10] There, he met the fateful group of prospectors who were in the process of discussing a need for horses. Also in the bar was this tale's version of Gotch Ear, not named, plus Davidson and an old Dutchman, described here as an experienced Indian fighter. With nothing else to lose, Adams threw in with the men by way of the fourteen horses he had left. Four days later, on August 20, 1864, the group left Maricopa Wells under the guidance of the half-Mexican half-Indian guide.

After about seven or eight days of travel, the group came upon the great bluff of a canyon, which "presented the appearance of an unbroken wall." The guide then led them to the secret door at the foot of the bluff and they followed the typical zigzag trail into the canyon. There, the elated miners discovered enough gold to keep them occupied even though the guide had told them that even more gold could be found elsewhere. At mention of the cabin, Johnston interceded to note that it was built above the waterfall. In his book, he noted, "Both [Captain Shaw] and my father were sure of that, although so far as I know, other versions of the story place it below [the falls]."[11]

Frontier era log cabin c.1908 on postcard.

In this version, upon the appearance of Chief Nana, the guide was called upon to act as an interpreter even though typically he'd already left by then. Through their interpreter, the men were told that Nana warned that so long as they did not go below the falls they would not be harmed. The men agreed to these terms, and Nana left. However, a few days later, Nana returned and was seen talking to the guide again. What they spoke of, the men did not know, but the guide asked for his pay and left soon after.

A few days later, the Dutchman spied the guide's horse being ridden by an Apache. At the same time, some of the miners were descending below the falls, where they found even greater gold. This greatly accelerated the wealth that they were accumulating, which some valued at just a little below $100,000. As supplies began to dwindle, Davidson ordered six men, including the Dutchman, to set off for Fort Wingate with some of the gold to purchase food and more tools for mining. On the sixth day, Davidson became concerned when the men did not return. He and Adams exited the canyon to find the men scalped and riddled with arrows. Strangely enough, among the bodies of the six men was that of one that they did not recognize, indicating that they had apparently decided to let a new member join their party. As usual, though, the Dutchman's body was not among the dead. Another interesting layer to this version was that Adams claimed that one of the dead had a premonition. Before he left, he had given Adams the name of his wife and also his address and had asked Adams to write to her if anything happened to him.

Adams and Davidson then buried the men best that they could under loose stones since no soil was available in the rocky canyon where they had been killed. Upon returning to the stream, they found their cabin in flames and the other miners there dead. Whereas usually Adams retrieved an especially large nugget from a special hiding place separate from the cabin, in this version he only attempted to do so: "After a long and torturous crawl that did not get him near the hidden nugget, he returned it to Davidson, and then to hit the trail for Fort Wingate."[12]

Things proceeded as usual, with the duo wandering the desert until they were picked up by a detachment of cavalry from Fort Wingate. With them were six Apache, and on the spot, an enraged Adams shot five of them dead and the sixth only survived because Adams' hammer clicked on an empty chamber. Adams was then arrested and returned to the fort with Davidson.[13] However, in this version, the captain who arrested Adams sympathized with him, knowing that Adams killed the Apache out of revenge. As such, he secretly left for Adams his own horse, plus food and water, so that he could escape. Johnston explained that "someone carelessly left [the guardhouse] unlocked one night" so that Adams could sneak away in the darkness.[14]

Adams made it back to San Diego, where he promised his wife that he would never attempt to find the canyon again. Fifteen years later at a Masonic meeting, he told his story of the lost gold to his Masonic brothers. Among the listeners was Captain Shaw and the rest, as they say, was history.

Chapter Notes

[1] *Albuquerque Tribune* (September 27, 1966).

[2] Published on July 2, 1927, the same *Herald* article even mentioned a variation where Adams escaped with two companions instead of just one. It was odd in that neither the Dutchman nor Davidson were mentioned, but instead a man named McCall who afterwards died in the Civil War.

[3] Bryan, "Off the Beaten Path," *Albuquerque Tribune* (September 27, 1966).

[4] Kemp and Dykes, *Cow Dust and Saddle Leather*, p.271.

[5] Ibid, p.272.

[6] The man known only as Cooley should not be confused with either James or Michael Cooney, the two brothers who mined the Mogollons and had a few connections with the Adams legend.

[7] This story utilized elements pertaining to two separate gold caches located within the Navajo Nation in New Mexico and Arizona. In the winter of 1890, a group of prospectors in search of the Adams Diggings did find gold in the Carrizo mountains, which is actually what the article was referring to. The article's reference to Navajos aiding the prospectors was likely lifted from the story of Adams' Cave, wherein Indian trader Henry Adams was taken by some Navajo friends to a gold cave on the reservation near Fort Defiance, Arizona.

[8] Phillips, "A Pilot's Opinion on the Lost Adams," *Gold!* (Fall 1975), p.25.

[9] Johnston, *Old Magdalena Cow Town*, p.111.

[10] Ibid, p.112.

[11] Ibid, p.114.

[12] Ibid, p.117.

[13] Davidson's fate was left up in the air in this version, although he was a free man and not under arrest when at Fort Wingate.

[14] Johnston, *Old Magdalena Cow Town*, p.118.

California prospector c.1850s.

3.

WHO WAS ADAMS?
THE MAN BEHIND THE MYTH

Perhaps as mysterious as the diggings themselves is the true identity of Adams. As W.C. Jameson surmised in his book *The Lost Canyon of Gold*, "No verifiable first name has ever been attributed to him, and no photograph of Adams has ever been found."[1] Just as there were many conflicting versions of the tale of Adams, so too were there contradictory versions of Adams himself. Though typically he lacked a first name in most of the renditions, a few bestowed initials upon him if nothing else, and others a full name, though those were admittedly rare.

Along the same lines, many have also wondered when and where Adams was born, when he died, and furthermore, if he was really a freighter or not. Due to the traditional Adams account being set during the Civil War, it makes sense to many that Adams would have been a soldier rather than a freighter. W.C. Jameson put forth the theory that perhaps Adams was really an outlaw from the East who had fled to the West to escape execution. "Others insist he came from Oregon, where he was a failed gold miner and entrepreneur, and a few documents exist that strongly suggest a connection between Adams and that state," Jameson went on to state.[2]

Lastly, there is even a possibility that the party of twenty-two men bore more than one member by the name of Adams. It was a common name and still is, so why couldn't there have been two Adams in the party, depending upon the size? In addition to that, there were several other Adams across the West who found separate caches of gold, further confusing the legend.

Needless to say, there's a lot to unravel when it comes to Adams. What will follow are the numerous conflicting accounts of his name, his character, and his life beyond the diggings in general.

Though sometimes used to portray Adams, this June 1955 *True West* cover depicted the Lost Dutchman treasure of Arizona.

Names Perhaps adding to the mystique of Adams is that mythologically speaking, he has no first name. Or, in the words of Dobie, "Like Adam, Adams seems to have had no 'front name.'"[3] Occasionally, yarn spinners would bestow a first name upon him, or lacking a full name, at least a mysterious set of initials. One *Old West* article gave him the adventurous first name of Buck, though I have a feeling that the author simply plucked it out of thin air.[4]

A letter written by Clark Rodgers of Grant County to the *Silver City Enterprise* in 1912 gave him the initials of A.V. Adams. Where Rodgers got these initials, or what they stood for, is unknown, but the name A.V. Adams did appear in two other newspaper accounts. The first was in an August 1886 article out of Albuquerque. Likewise, R.C. Patterson, who knew Adams firsthand, referred to him as A.V. Adams in the *Socorro Chieftain* of January 9, 1904. Conversely, Magdalena lawman Bob Lewis, who also met Adams, was certain his name was Edward Adams. Langford Johnston, who got his information from Captain Shaw, claimed the full name was John H. Adams in *Old Magdalena Cow Town*.

While these were all hearsay remembrances, researcher and prospector Jack Purcell may well have unearthed the true name of Adams. Purcell found records of a soldier, Charles H. Adams from Marysville, California, who was part of the California Column. Specifically, he was enlisted in Company D of the First Cavalry Regiment and began his enlistment on September 21, 1861, and served at Fort West and Fort Craig in 1863. Purcell also found records showing that Adams was discharged on August 14, 1864. Considering that many Adams tales took place in August 1864, the dates added up rather well.

Ultimately, while it's certainly intriguing to ponder the man's real name, as it stands, the lack of a first name only adds to Adams' legend.

Physical Descriptions Just what Adams looked like is another contested issue. Naturally, he was portrayed as a typical prospector in artwork, but what did he really look like? As with his name, accounts varied. One of the best and most vivid descriptions of Adams, assuming that it was accurate, came from the lips of B.D. Nichols, an El Paso mining man who claimed to have met Adams in 1883 in California. Nichols described Adams as a "big, portly, pink-faced man with hair as white as paper. He was more than six feet tall and must have weighed 230 pounds. The kind of man you look at twice any place."[5] At that time, Nichols said that Adams was already more than 80 years old.

In direct opposition to this, in *True Tales of the American Southwest* by Howard Bryan, the author stated that the inhabitants of Milligan's Plaza described Adams as "a short, slender man, with white hair and a short, gray beard, who spent much of his time spinning yarns about his lost gold while drinking heavily in local saloons."[6] Dobie also quoted a few old-timers from Milligan's Plaza along the San Francisco River, which Adams frequented in the 1870s. "The way his long, shaggy eyebrows hung down over his eyes made you think of an old Spanish mare with matted mane covering her face," Dobie wrote.[7] If this was the famous folklorist's artistic license at work, or an accurate description, is anyone's guess. However, it also lined up with the description given of Adams in 1892 by Washie Jones in *Cow Dust and Saddle Leather*. In it, Adams was described by Jones as a "very old man" who "presented a pathetic figure... Weeping and trying to describe the country near his rich placer mine."[8]

Discrepancies regarding his stature aside, Adams seemed to fit the bill of the quintessential Old West prospector.

Broadway Street in Los Angeles c.1893-1895.

Adams' Life Outside of the Diggings Naturally, most accounts of Adams focused on his life as they pertained to the diggings, without much attention given to his prior history. Dobie claimed that Adams was born in Rochester, New York, on July 10, 1829, which would have made him thirty-five years old when he discovered the diggings. It is thought that Dobie's birthplace and birthdate for Adams came from Captain Shaw. Backing this up was Langford Johnston's *Old Magdalena Cow Town*, in which it was related that Captain Shaw told Johnston's father the history of Adams. Johnston's summation of Adam's early life via Shaw was as follows:

> **TO WORK A LOST MINE.**
>
> Believer in the Adams Treasure. Eliciting Backing.
>
> KANSAS CITY, Mo., May 12.—L. S. Gordon of Wingate, N. M., is in this city endeavoring to organize a company to open the Navajo reservation in New Mexico for the reason that he has a certain clue to the famous lost Adams mine.
>
> Three years ago "Yank" Adams, an old miner, walked into Wingate and told a story of a wonderful gold mine he had discovered in the mountains of the Navajo reservation, and showed specimens of ore of wonderful richness. He would not tell where the mine was except to some one who would advance him money to develop it and overcome the Indians, who will allow no white man within their territory.
>
> One morning he was found dead, probably murdered for plans or maps which no one found, and since then the mine has been lost.

The Boston Daily Globe of May 13, 1890, which also referred to Adams as "Yank".

John H. Adams was born in Rochester, New York, on July 10, 1829. Even as a schoolboy he was interested in reading of Arizona and New Mexico and of the Indians and cowboys, and he wanted to see that mysterious and beautiful country. How he made a livelihood is not known, but he married and had three children. In the late 50s he sailed from New York to San Diego, California, and engaged in freighting. He may have had some money, but it is certain that he was able to get credit for more, and he bought two wagons and fourteen head of horses.[9]

Adams being born in New York also aligned with some accounts that referred to him as a "northerner". According to Mr. L.S. Gordon from Fort Wingate, "He gave his name as Adams, and the peculiar twang of his voice gave him the title of 'Yank,' by which nickname he was called by the miners."[10]

In strict contrast to this was a statement made by R.C. Patterson, who alleged in 1897 that "Adams was a southern man" and that "he couldn't cuss the government as he wanted to in California" so "he went to Arizona."

Whether a Southerner or a Northerner, Adams for certain spent much of his life in Los Angeles, California, with his wife and children. While Johnston's account of Adams had him leaving behind a family to hunt the gold, Washie Jones implied that Adams was unmarried when he endured his famous adventure. It was only after his return home to California that he married and began a family, though most accounts already gave Adams his family.

As to what Adams did for a living post-diggings, many sources, including Dobie, stated that Adams ran a secondhand furniture shop in Los Angeles and, following that, a livery stable. (One account, from Silver City resident Jack Fleming, placed the livery stable in San Diego as opposed to Los Angeles, though.) Wherever his business was, Dobie claimed Adams was almost always broke. The only other author to mention Adams' California business in depth was Harry Sinclair Drago, who wrote in *Lost Bonanzas* that "His secondhand store on lower Main Street became a gathering place for desert rats and hardrock miners from Death Valley and the Panamints."[11]

What became of Adams' shop, or his alleged family for that matter, is unknown, but most accounts had Adams dying in the year 1886, which leads us to our next matter of contention...

Adams' Death The typical account of Adams' death was that he had suffered a heart attack while searching for the diggings in the mountains of New Mexico. The weakened Adams had been carried to a nearby railroad depot and took the train home to California, where he died on September 21st. There are, of course, many accounts to the contrary.

Though first recounted by Dobie in *Apache Gold & Yaqui Silver*, Langford Johnston gave a more detailed version in *Old Magdalena Cow Town*. Unlike other iterations of the tale, with Adams simply trying and failing to find the diggings, according to Johnston, they had rediscovered the most important landmarks and were on the cusp of reentering the canyon:

A doctor had warned Adams that his heart was bad, and he had symptoms of trouble but was so excited over at last being on the right track that he would not heed Shaw's insistence that they turn back. Before they reached the little door opening into the canyon containing the gold, Adams suffered a heart attack and Shaw took him home. In September 1886, he died at San Diego.[12]

> ### The Romance of Mining.
> A few days since, says the Socorro Chieftain, Dr. Brown, a gentleman aged about 60 years, arrived here from Phœnix, A. T., for the purpose of examining some mines in the Magdalenas. Doctor Brown claims that he was personally acquainted with the man Adams, after whom the famous Adams diggings were named, and gives the following story as told to him by Adams about two years ago, at Los Angeles where the doctor called on Adams, who died about two months afterward.

The *El Paso Times* of June 2, 1886
claimed Adams died in 1884.

Contrary to Adam's September 1886 death was an article from the *Daily Republican* of June 23, 1886, which claimed that Adams had "died a little while ago." Perhaps, though, it actually alluded to his heart attack suffered in New Mexico that same year, and the paper merely presumed he was by now dead. The article also stated that when Adams died in Los Angeles, he left behind several "valuable charts of the country he had traversed" as well as "plans for further campaigns."[13]

John A. Glass, a First Lieutenant in the Sixth Cavalry, claimed another demise for Adams. According to what Glass heard, "The original Adams was shot in a drunken brawl and on his death-bed told of a mine of vast richness that he had discovered and located."[14] Another Adams deathbed encounter came courtesy of a man identified only as "Johnson" by the *El Paso Herald* in an August 13, 1927, article. According to Johnson, "who still lives just south of the malpais," only two years after returning to California, Adams came back to New Mexico. Johnson said,

> The party went into the malpais region from St. John's, as I remember it, only to be snowbound by a big storm in the spring of that year. While they were waiting for the snow to go away, Adams was taken with inflammatory rheumatism which later developed into partial paralysis.[15]

While he was in that condition and not long before he died, Johnson went to visit him. Adams told Johnson as best he could how to find the gold but added that he would never find it, as it would be next to impossible for anyone who had not been there to find the place.[16]

Lastly, there was even one source who claimed that Adams actually died during the massacre, and that a successor by the same name later took up his mantle...

Adams the Impostor? During the 1870s and 1880s, it wasn't uncommon for practical jokers to tell tall tales about such things as the Lost Adams Diggings. Some undoubtedly pretended to be Adams for their own amusement, while others might have impersonated Adams to get grubstaked just long enough to get by. Others may have simply enjoyed the attention that being a celebrity warranted. "Like the names of John Wilkes Booth, Billy the Kid and other notabilities, [Adams' name] has been assumed by impostors, bringing confusion both to his reputation and the plain story he originally told," J. Frank Dobie noted.[17]

Along those lines, an interesting theory as to Adams was put forth in Howard Bryan's "Off the Beaten Path" column. The source of the story was Wilbur B. Cassady, who claimed that Adams was never Adams to begin with. Bryan wrote in his September 27, 1966, column that Cassady claimed "that the Adams of the Lost Adams Diggings was among the prospectors killed by Indians at the mine, and that the Adams who later searched for the lost mine was not the Adams of the Lost Adams Diggings. Confusing, isn't it?"

This idea allegedly came from Captain Shaw, who told Cassady that "the real Mr. Adams" was killed during the Indian attack at the mine and that "a roving cowboy named Adams later came forth pretending to be the discoverer of the Lost Adams Diggings and became quite a hero."

Cassady also implied that Captain Shaw could have been considered the "real Adams" in the sense that he was actually the lone survivor of the attack. Cassady told Bryan, "I do not claim that C.G. Shaw was that sole survivor of the Adams Diggings massacre, but if not he certainly knew who was or he would not have known that the sole survivor left the gold nugget at the Derfey Wells ranch…"[18]

Not only was the possibility that Adams was dead before the story could ever be spread put forth, but so was the idea that the canyon was rediscovered by a separate man named Adams. Old time El Paso resident William Donothan claimed that there was a second man named Adams, Joe Adams, who in either 1885 or 1886 led a party of six, comprising of both men and women, to the canyon. Like the original group, they were guided by way of a "half-breed" who "had a map he had obtained in some mysterious manner."[19] There, they were also attacked by the Apache and had to flee. Actually, in the case of this incident, Adams and his compatriots were all killed but two. The lone survivors comprised a man named Kelmere and one of the women. Though both were wounded in the attack, they managed to flee to Socorro.[20]

Also adding to the confusion was the tale of a Henry Adams, who found gold on the Navajo reservation near Fort Defiance. This Adams was an Indian trader who, after winning the confidence of a few Navajo, was taken to a golden cave hidden within a canyon. However, Henry Adams never claimed to be the Adams of the Adams Diggings, and newspapers simply confused the two due to their both having the same names and being associated with a lost gold strike.

ADAMS THE LIAR

This article, published in the *Arizona Weekly Enterprise* of June 28, 1890, denounced Adams as nothing but a liar:

Adams Diggings a Myth.

J. F. Williams, a hearty old gentleman, 63 years of age, as straight as an arrow, with a countenance as open and honest as the day is long, is spending a few days in the city. Mr. Williams passed through this country in '49 and located in California. He first met Adams, of the famous Adams diggings, in 1859. At that time Adams had never been to this country. In '60 or '61 Adams visited Tucson, and sold some property belonging to his wife. He then settled on the peninsula, and never did return to this country until about '80.

"Then, the story is a myth?" asked the reporter.

"The whole business is a lie," quietly remarked the old gentleman. "I know what I am talking about, and I have mighty little use for a man who has caused so many good people trouble. Adams is a counterfeit, and I can prove it by a number of good citizens in Los Angeles county. The truth is not in him sir, and never was. May the Lord have mercy on such," remarked the old gentleman with a sigh.

Adams Goes Insane A few iterations of the Adams tale claimed that Adams went insane in his later years, either from the Apache massacre or from not being able to find the diggings again. An article in the *Clifton Copper Era* of December 9, 1909, related how Adams "went insane and was never able to locate the exact place again." This was also stated by Jason Baxter, an ex-soldier who first met Adams in Arizona. "He was O.K. then, but later when I saw him at Pinos Altos, he seemed a kind of loco," Baxter told James A. McKenna. "Indian experience had somehow affected his mind," Baxter surmised.[21] Furthermore, as far as Baxter was concerned, the diggings might've been located within the confines of Adams' mind alone. Likewise, B.D. Nichols, who met Adams in

California in his later years, felt the entire tale was completely made up and "the obsession of a diseased mind."[22]

Another of those who claimed to know Adams firsthand appeared in the *Boston Sunday Post's* article, "A Lost Gold Mine," printed on September 19, 1897. The man, who went unnamed, was a current blacksmith in Duncan, Arizona, and a former prospector. "I knew old man Adams intimately and always believed him," the man stated but also confirmed stories that Adams was thought to be loco. "A good many doubted him, and said the old man was crazy; but I saw the gold he brought out with him—big, coarse flakes—no dust." He continued,

> Although at first a good many believed him and went back with him to find the diggings, after a while, with so many failures to locate the place, nearly everyone turned a deaf ear to his story. There's no doubt the old man got a little crazy towards the last, when he found he could convince no one of the truth of his story.

Adams the Soldier In the 1920s, a favorite source for Adams tales in the *El Paso Herald* was old-timer William Donothan, who told some real whoppers on the diggings. Among them were rumors of outlaws guarding the canyon as opposed to Apaches, a Spanish gold mine there, and that there were two Adams, not one. However, to his credit, Donothan put forth one theory about Adams that might hold water. Donothan, who was a sergeant in the Seventh Cavalry, postulated that the original Adams party of the 1860s consisted not of prospectors, but of soldiers. This opinion is shared by some of the more credible and knowledgeable Adams enthusiasts today.

As stated earlier, Jack Purcell found records of a soldier from the California Column by the name of Charles H. Adams from Marysville, California. Not only that, this Adams even served in the Southwest around the time that story of the diggings was supposed to have taken place. Specifically, he was enlisted in Company D, the First Cavalry Regiment of the California Column. He began his enlistment on September 21, 1861, and served at Fort West and Fort Craig in 1863. Purcell also found records showing that Adams was discharged on August 14, 1864. Further adding to the evidence is the fact that a Davidson, in this case Solomon Davidson, and a John Brewer were discharged on the same day. The time and place also aligned with a few other Adams players, one those being Dr. D.B. Sturgeon. If you'll recall, Sturgeon was the doctor who treated Adams and Davidson after their ordeal, and records showed that he was in southern New Mexico in 1863. So, too, was Jacob Snively, likely the real Dutchman. Snively was hanging around Pinos Altos at the time and was frequently seen bringing in gold from a secret location.

Civil War soldiers marching in formation.

However, if Adams was a military man, why then did he claim to be a freighter? And if Brewer and Adams were fellow soldiers, why did Brewer act as though he met Adams by chance along the trail? Jack Purcell speculated in his book that perhaps Adams, Brewer, and Davidson "shared a dark secret."[23] That was why Adams would've fabricated the story that he was a freighter rather than a soldier (or perhaps a horse thief). It's also undeniably odd how Adams often changed the other lone survivor of his tale. Ofttimes it was Davidson but other times it was the Dutchman, and in some, Adams escaped by his lonesome with no companions at all.

Another problem was that there were naturally many Adams running around the West during the Civil War. Another of those that Purcell unearthed was Captain W.C. Adams of Company C of Fort Davis. This Adams was a Confederate, as opposed to the other Adams with the California Column. Likewise, Jacob Snively was himself a captain in the Confederate Army for a time.

Ultimately, due to the time frame of the Civil War, plus the suspicious discrepancies in Adam's varying accounts, the idea of a party of soldiers entering the canyon in 1864, then later disguising their stories to protect their identities, seems to hold water.

Chapter Notes

---

[1] Jameson, *Lost Canyon of Gold*, p.3.

[2] Ibid, pp.3-4.

[3] Dobie, *Apache Gold & Yaqui Silver*, p.5

[4] "Apache Gold" by George Dillon, covered in the next chapter.

[5] *El Paso Herald* (July 2, 1927).

[6] Bryan, *True Tales of the American Southwest*, p.46.

[7] Dobie, *Apache Gold & Yaqui Silver*, p.40.

[8] Kemp and Dykes, *Cow Dust and Saddle Leather*, p.273.

[9] Johnston, *Old Magdalena Cow Town*, p.110. It's important to note that Johnston didn't publish his memoirs until the 1980s. It's possible he may have even used *Apache Gold & Yaqui Silver* to help him fill in a few blanks regarding Adams. It wasn't uncommon, for instance, for old-timers who knew Billy the Kid well to list wrong dates and falsehoods about the outlaw that they had picked up from books and articles over the years when they were being interviewed for the FWP in the 1930s. Also, the idea of Adams as a schoolboy in the late 1830s and early 1840s reading about New Mexico seems like a romantic notion thrown in just a flavor the tale. However, the name and story given to Johnston, it should be noted, aligned with an account given by one of Adams's alleged descendants many years later. See the entry on *Die Rich Here!* in the bibliography for more on that.

[10] *Fort Worth Daily Gazette* (May 10, 1890).

[11] Drago, *Lost Bonanzas*, pp.207-208.

[12] Johnston, *Old Magdalena Cow Town*, p.119.

[13] Interestingly the same article said that he had been taken to the diggings by a "party of Indians with whom he was on good terms and

with three or four friends he worked the lead until they were driven off by hostiles."

[14] "IN PURSUIT OF VICTORIO'S BAND," *Grand Rapids Wood County Tribune* (February 27,1890).

[15] "Prospector spends 40 years hunting lost Adams Diggin's," *El Paso Herald* (August 13, 1927).

[16] Ibid.

[17] Dobie, *Apache Gold & Yaqui Silver,* p.5.

[18] See "The Wilbur B. Cassady Account" on pp.39-40.

[19] "El Pasoan Plans Search for Lost Adams Diggin's," *El Paso Herald* (July 16, 1927).

[20] Randle, *Lost Gold & Buried Treasure,* p.32.

[21] McKenna, *Black Range Tales,* p.32.

[22] *El Paso Herald* (July 2, 1927).

[23] Unlike many Adams experts who focused solely on finding the canyon, Purcell put forth quite a bit of effort into finding the real Adams. In his search, Purcell came along an Adams enthusiast from California in the early 1990s who claimed to have found military records of Adams being rescued by a military regiment. Despite his best efforts, the man would never share these records with Purcell and as such their existence is suspect.

4.

PULP ADAMS
GOLDEN WEST TALES

Around the same time that television Westerns, like *Gunsmoke*, became popular, Western magazines also rose to prominence. Though publications like *Frontier Times* had existed since 1923, it was magazines like *True West*, first published in 1953, that really kicked off the craze. *Real West* followed in 1957, and not long after, *Frontier Times* was revamped as a companion to *True West*. *Old West*, *Golden West*, and others followed suit in the mid-1960s. It was these magazines that took up the mantle of Adams and turned him into a pulp hero of sorts.

The first article I found giving Adams the pulp hero treatment was from an obscure magazine called *True Western Adventure*. "Treasure of Massacre Mine," written by Horace Baily Brown, was published in the February 1959 issue and began with a bold teaser statement reading, "'Stay off the mesas,' the Indian chief had warned them. But the nuggets on the mesas were big and the prospectors were only human. The nuggets are still there. And so are the prospectors."

To delve into the "meat and potatoes" of the article, Brown gives Adams the first name of Jim and begins in the late spring of 1864. It also portrays Adams as a heavy drinker:

> [Adams] had only a few miles to get to Tucson and Tucson was full of saloons which Jim Adams liked more

than a little. But that night found Jim with a full supply of his own whiskey and when he reached Gila Bend he decided it would taste just as good there as it would in Tucson – and it would taste good sooner.[1]

Shortly after suffering the Apache raid on his camp, Adams enters the Pima village. Instead of joining a group of prospectors there, Adams barters with some Pima braves to help him track down the Apache who stole his goods. The braves agree to do so in return for half of his remaining horses. Adams and the braves set out along the San Pedro River and catch up with the renegade Apache who flee at the sight of the numerous Pima men with Adams. Adams regains his lost money from the Apache, and then bargains with one unnamed Pima brave to be his guide back to Tucson, as Adams seems to have lost his way.

On their way back to Tucson, Adams and the Pima guide encounter the fateful prospectors. The men are examining some gold ore when the Pima guide informs them that he can take them to a canyon where there are gold nuggets "as big as buzzard eggs."[2] From there, off the group goes to what the Pima guide calls the "land of never never rain."

Oddly, Brown goes on to name several members of the expedition which he claims Adams named in later accounts. However, as usual, many of these are just strange variations of the existing party names and it's unknown if Brown had access to special information, or if some of the names he simply plucked from thin air. Among Brown's cast of Adams characters are "Jay Davidson, John Brewer, also known as John Wingate, Roy Peters, a surly German known only as The Dutchman, Bill Foley, Armand Hostetter, Slim Wakefield and Curly Rogers."[3]

Brown has the men travel for ten days through New Mexico until finally arriving in Apache County, Arizona. Shortly after this, they reach the land of never never rain.[4] On the twentieth day, they sight the entrance to the canyon, which in this version has cliffs reaching upwards of 1,000 feet high. As for the Pima guide, he abruptly exits the story by stating that it's "bad medicine stealing red man's gold."[5]

While Brown characterizes his version of Gotch Ear as the stereotypical stilted-English-speaking Indian, he portrays the Dutchman as the unlikable villain of the piece. When Adams and Brewer start doling out orders, it is only the Dutchman who tries to buck their authority. At one point, Adams even draws his revolver on him, and later Adams catches the Dutchman stuffing his pockets with extra gold nuggets.

> "Look, Dutchman," [Adams] said, "from now on you'll help with the cabin instead of pannin' gold."
> The Dutchman agreed when he saw the others were on Adam's side, but the surly, evil look on his face boded ill for the mule skinner.[6]

Uncredited illustration of the Dutchman finding gold in "Treasure of Massacre Mine."

Rather remarkably, the completed cabin ends up being large enough for all twenty-two men to sleep within and, as usual, comes complete with the gold cache beneath the hearth. In this iteration, all the miners get greedy; secretly hiding gold nuggets. However, so much gold is accumulating beneath the hearth that Adams and Brewer decide to let the matter slide.

The villainous tribe of Indians enter the story soon after. However, they are not identified as Apache, and therefore Chief Nana makes no appearance. Brewer, described as a former soldier and Indian fighter in this version, goes to speak with them. Rather than warning them not to go beyond the waterfall, this chief cautions them not to "invade the surrounding area outside and the high mesas above the cliffs."

Two weeks later, the Dutchman voices his desire to leave early. Adams and Brewer warn him that he can't make it alone, but the Dutchman decides to take his chances. Though set up as something of a villain, the Dutchman receives no villainous ending and simply rides off with his gold never to be seen again. Later, in June, Brewer sets out with the supply team for Fort Wingate whilst at the same time some of the miners begin frequenting the mesas. Eventually Adams and Davidson decide to go out looking for the supply party, and instead of coming upon a mass slaughter, they discover one body at a time along the trail, often scalped and riddled with arrows.

In an interesting departure, Adams and Davidson return to camp not to find a massacre, but to see their fellow miners returning from the mesa, where they were ambushed by the Indians and got away. Oddly, the miners decide to stay in camp while Adams and Davidson go out to look for Brewer a second time. Again they find no trace of Brewer and only his dead companions. From outside of the canyon, they begin hearing gunfire and wild shouts. Knowing that their camp is under fire, they rush back.

For the most part, the rest of the story is typical in that Adams and Davidson come upon the scene of the massacre, try to excavate some gold from the ruined cabin, and then flee. Where Brown deviates is in actually picking up the trail of Brewer for a change. Brown chronicles Brewer hiding out amidst the rocks, unaware that Adams and Davidson are nearby and then has him commence his odyssey through the desert, wandering along the Rio Grande River until he's taken in by a friendly group of Indians.

Meanwhile, in a pulpy dramatic twist, Davidson goes insane on the trail:

As the days passed Davidson's mind began to play tricks with him. He took a violent hatred to Adams and tried to kill him on several occasions. One day he ate a handful of strange berries and became seriously ill. For a week he hovered between life and death, finally recovering sufficient strength to go on.[7]

Odder yet, Brown doesn't include the dramatic confrontation between Adams and the Apache that had surrendered at Fort Wingate. (Perhaps he realized he had reached his desired word count and skipped it?) Instead, Adams peaceably moves on for Santa Fe without incident and eventually makes it back to Los Angeles. And with that, what appears to be the first pulp iteration of Adams comes to an end.

The next article to give Adams the pulp treatment was written by Stuart Whitehouse for the November 1964 issue of *Golden West*. As the title "Charlie Adams and the Valley of Gold" suggests, Whitehouse gives Adams a first name as a way of humanizing him for the reader. Along these same lines, Adams has conversations with his horse, Belle, on the trail:

"There's Gila Bend just ahead, Belle," he told the mare. "And we're only a week out of Tucson. Fresh water for all of you tonight. Keep this up, and we'll be in Los Angeles in a month."[8]

Whitehouse notes that Adams couldn't have been more wrong, as he was "about to be hurled into one of the most violent true adventures in the history of the Old West."[9]

Whitehouse keeps the tale set in the summer of 1864, but places Adams' birthplace as Philadelphia for some reason as opposed to New York. But, in keeping with Adams' traditional birthdate of around 1830, this Adams is still 35 years old. Whitehouse describes him as "lean and leathery"[10] with long hair and a mustache. As Adams beds down with Belle for the night, he delivers some expository dialogue about how he's hauling $2,000 in gold pieces and "not Rebel Paper," a crafty allusion to the Civil War, which many Adams accounts ignored. Adams then laments how the Johnny Rebs have pulled out of Arizona, and perhaps when the war is over he'll buy a ranch. (Apparently no wife and kids for this iteration of Adams yet.)

This old Frederick Remington illustration was used as the main header of the article.

The same story plays out as usual, with the Apache diversion to get Adams away from his camp. However, this craftier version of Adams figures out it's a diversion unlike his counterparts and heads back for camp at once. Afterwards, the down-on-his-luck Adams heads for a Pima village where he encounters a group of about twenty men led by "a huge bearded man named Samuel Davidson."[11] They too suffered an Indian raid that cost them some of their horses, which is what leads them to offer to buy Adams' remaining stock.

There is an Indian guide in this version, too, but Whitehouse must have misread or misremembered Dobie, for in his version Gotch Ear is renamed Notch Ear. That said, the character serves the same function, leading the men to the "canyon of gold—and death."[12] Along the way, Adams also notes how the trip might be safer due to federal troops having moved into Arizona, the hope being that they might keep the warring Apache subdued. On that note, Whitehouse is among those who decided to place the diggings in Northeastern Arizona in the area of the Navajo Reservations. As in *Mackenna's Gold*, Whitehouse even has the men trek through the red rocks of Canyon de Chelly to reach the twin peaks.

Notch Ear gets them to the titular valley of gold, where the men nosily rejoice at the sight of gold. Adams rewards Notch Ear with an extra blanket and instructions for their interpreter to tell him that "he's an honest man" before parting ways. Before departing, Notch Ear issues a warning to not be so jubilant in their revelry, for the nearby Apache may hear them and come to investigate. Particularly fearful of that warning is Whitehouse's version of the Dutchman, who he describes as a husky young man from Munich and names Otto Geisert. Afraid to linger too long, the Dutchman doesn't agree to share in the gold or help build the log cabin.

Nana and his band come calling as usual but are friendlier than Notch Ear made them out to be. Nana says the men are welcome to harvest as many of the yellow stones as they like so long as they don't venture onto the Apache campground above the falls. Nana issues an additional ultimatum, though, that the men must leave before the first snowfall.

After construction of the cabin, supplies wane and a party exits the canyon to get provisions under the leadership of George Brewer. Along with the supply party is the Dutchman, who wishes to leave with his gold and his scalp still intact. In their absence, the men begin venturing above the falls. Though Adams warns against this, he too finds an especially huge nugget that he thinks he will one day fasten to a watch chain.[13] (In the same paragraph, Whitehouse either adds some unique flourishes from his writer's mind or publishes heretofore unknown anecdotes on the gold, for he claims that the other men found a nugget in the shape of a bear, and another, ominously, in the shape of a small human skull.)

One day, as Adams and Davidson total the gold under the hearth at around $100,000, they become worried about the supply group and decide to ride out and look for them. They find the men's mutilated, scalped remains outside of the canyon sans Brewer and the Dutchman. The duo return to camp to find it in flames as 200 Apache attack. Adams and

Davidson then spend the rest of the night hiding in terror as Apaches with "wet scalps dangling at [their] belts" walk past them.[14]

The two men escape once the Apache have left without the gold cache beneath the hearth, but with the large nugget Adams had hidden elsewhere. The rest of the tale is the same story for the most part, with the men being rescued by a detachment of men from Fort Wingate. Davidson returns to Michigan, where he dies soon after, though not before leaving behind a map that Whitehouse says was used in an aerial search in 1931.

Next came "Apache Gold" by George Dillon, published in a 1966 issue of *Old West*, which gave Adams the bold first name of Buck. In Dillon's story, Buck Adams is coming out of the California Gold Rush with seven other prospectors for Arizona Territory in 1862. Although I assume this was just artistic license to better visualize his tale, Dillon describes Adams as "a big rugged-looking man with sandy hair and a square, stubborn chin" who spoke in something of a drawl.[15] Dillon also paints Adams as a devil-may-care protagonist, scorning the warnings of a fellow prospector not to hunt the Apache gold:

> "Them Apaches is plain hell," the sutler cautioned. "You never see 'em till they're on you—then it's too late!"
> Buck hitched up his trousers and spat contemptuously into the sandbox under the pot-bellied stove. "We been up against Cheyennes and Comanches, so I reckon we won't worry none about Apaches."[16]

Although Dillon's version of the tale eschews Gotch Ear, it does include the Dutchman, who Dillon gives the name of Hein Hoffman to. As in some other versions, the Dutchman sees the writing on the canyon wall, or rather the Indian smoke signals in this case, and decides to leave with what little gold he has before trouble starts. Actually, Dillon includes two Dutchmen in his tale, as there is another named Dutch Brandel who observes the massacre from afar with Adams. After the

Apaches kill four of their comrades, Adams and Brandel wander the desert for twelve days and nights, subsisting on prairie dogs.

Al Martin Napoletano's artwork for "Apache Gold," reprinted in the 1969 *Gold!* Annual.

Eventually the duo comes across a procession of soldiers from Fort West, who have with them eight Apache prisoners. Adams immediately recognizes the garb of a dead prospector, Steve O'Connor, being worn by an Apache brave. In a rage, Adams snatches a rifle from one of the soldiers and threatens to shoot the Apache before two of the soldiers wrestle him to the ground.

Adams and Brandel are taken to Fort West with the soldiers, where an embittered Adams laments the fact that the Apache prisoners will probably never be executed for their crimes. Adams tries to entice his Dutch companion to steal horses, rifles, and other provisions from the soldiers to return to the canyon. However, Brandel is too afraid and takes a job herding cattle instead, so Adams decides to return to the canyon alone. To do so, he steals the commandant's horse and some provisions, hiding them in a nearby gully. Then, with two stolen pistols, Adams sneaks into the stockade holding the Apache and massacres them all. "Buck, with a wild yell, leaped in among them, firing from both pistols. The Apaches tried to fight him off with knife and club, but they had little chance before two blazing six-guns," Dillon wrote dramatically, then adds that Adams clubbed the remaining two Apache to death with the butt of his pistol.

Apache prisoners in Tucson, Arizona.
(Wittemann Collection, Library of Congress.)

Bruised and bleeding from the fight, Adams then makes a daring escape from the fort as it stirs to life from all the commotion he just caused. Dillon makes Adams a competent action hero by having him create a false trail leading westward before doubling back and concealing his tracks to lead the troops on a wild goose chase. But, it's not just the cavalry after Adams. Somehow the Apache know of their recently murdered brethren and are after Adams as well.

Lieutenant Emory, named after a real historical figure, then leads the hunt for Adams and manages to find him at a spot called Lost Creek.[17] Adams skillfully evades the gunfire of the troops to gallop into the desert, where he is accosted by a group of Apaches waiting in ambush:

Near sunset he rode into an Apache ambush. The Indians had smeared themselves with dust and humped like rocks beside the trail. But the setting sun betrayed them, highlighting a savage countenance for Buck's watchful eyes.

He snapped a shot at the Indian and spurred his horse. A dozen rocks came to life and sent death winging at him. But, blasting with both pistols, he fought through the ambush, taking, however, a painful flesh wound in the arm.[18]

Adams escapes to a rocky crevice, but not before riding his horse to death. As he observes Apache smoke signals, he decides that he can wait a few years to return to the canyon of gold. Miraculously, he evades the army and the Apache all the way back to San Francisco, where he boards a ship for South Africa, vowing to return one day for his lost gold.

Dillon concludes his story by describing Adams as a fugitive for twenty years, "living in distant lands, but always dreaming of his lost horde of gold."[19] He returns to America in 1883, having heard that the Apache had finally settled down and that he had long been forgotten by the army. Unfortunately for Adams, the land had changed in the last twenty years, with familiar landmarks too altered to recognize. Dillon then claims that Adams lived into the 20th century, reaching 93 years of age. Dillon's article concluded:

> Perhaps, if you whizzed through Arizona in your car a few decades ago, you saw him, plodding across the desert with his burro. An old, old man he was, with a long gray beard and time-bent shoulders, but still seeing, in his mind's eye, Fortune's warm golden smile, and still stubbornly refusing to believe that she had cast him aside.[20]

Ultimately, all three of these pastiches seem like rough passes at a Lost Adams adventure novel. Actually, it's too bad that one of them didn't endeavor to make their story into a full-length novel, or barring that, at least a novella.

Chapter Notes

[1] Brown, "Massacre Mine," *True Western Adventure* (February 1959), p.11.
[2] Ibid, p.12.
[3] Ibid.
[4] Even though Brown had places the men in Arizona, he still has them trek through the lava beds of the malpais, now apparently in Arizona in his version.
[5] Brown, "Massacre Mine," *True Western Adventure* (February 1959), p.13.
[6] Ibid.
[7] Ibid, p.76.
[8] Whitehouse, "Charlie Adams," *Golden West* (November 1964), p.32.
[9] Ibid.
[10] Ibid, p.33.
[11] Ibid.
[12] Ibid, p.50.
[13] I find this particularly interesting, because I thought Howard Bryan was the first writer to unearth tales of an Adams nugget being forged into a watch in a September 1966 edition of his "Off the Beaten Path" column. Whitehouse's article predates the column by about two years. Is it just a coincidence, or did Whitehouse hear a similar story?
[14] Whitehouse, "Charlie Adams," *Golden West* (November 1964), p.52.
[15] Dillon, "Apache Gold," *Old West*, p.38.
[16] Ibid.
[17] Lieutenant W.H. Emory was a real man who published the book *Notes of a Military Reconnaissance from Fort Leavenworth in Kansas to San Diego, California*. The mention of Emory strongly suggests that Dillon's main source in building his version of the story was the 1933 book *Lost Mines of the Great Southwest* by John D. Mitchell. I say this because Mitchell in particular made mention of Emory in his book. However, in Mitchell's account, Emory never crossed paths with Adams. Furthermore, Emory's book, which mentioned a story similar to Adams' but sans Adams himself, was published in 1848, well before the Adams adventure was thought to take place. See the chapter "Antecedents to Adams" for more on this.
[18] Dillon, "Apache Gold," *Old West*, pp.39/66.
[19] Ibid, p.66.
[20] Ibid.

5.

HIDDEN CANYON

LOST WORLD OF THE SOUTHWEST

C onsidering its status as a hidden land of death, gold, and adventure, Sno-Ta-Hay Canyon could probably qualify as a "lost world" of sorts. Among its more unbelievable attributes are strange landmarks, megalithic monoliths, ancient ruins, and even supernatural visions.[1] For that matter, *Mackenna's Gold* certainly fit the mold of a "Lost World" adventure in the form of a Western, as it was essentially a quest movie to a lost land. And though the real Lost Adams canyon was most certainly not as large as the one portrayed in the aforementioned film, it was, by most accounts, quite fantastic.

As in any adventure story, the way to the canyon was peppered with unique landmarks. Some routes—like that of Jake Schaeffer, another Dutchman who may have rediscovered the canyon—sported a mountain with the face of a woman on it. Another route featured the adventurously named "Island Mountain." Adams hunter Jason Baxter almost likened it to the ruins of an ancient civilization during his description of it in *Black Range Tales*:

> "That's Island Mountain, or Lone Mountain to the northeast. Don't it put you in mind of pictures you've seen of the pyramids of Egypt? After we passed through the natural gateway I told you about before, we'll soon be in the gulch of the Lost Diggings."[2]

"As I neared the Island Mountain the plants got weird," Baxter also remembered. He elaborated that there "were immense sotols and the largest cacti I have ever seen" in the area as well. "I could see mirages off to the east, and once in a while a salt laguna."[3]

Jack Purcell thinks "Island Mountain" could have been Escudilla Mountain located near the Arizona/New Mexico state line. If so, Escudilla Mountain has some interesting history worth recounting, as it was thought to be named by Coronado's conquistadors as they searched for the Seven Cities of Gold. It was also the haunt of outlaws in the 1880s, such as members of the James Gang.

While Island Mountain is mostly relative to Baxter, common to all accounts were two peaks within sight of the canyon. These peaks had some mystical qualities, as it turned out, with some claiming that they could only be seen at certain times of the year. Notably, an aerial search over the malpais for the diggings in 1927 turned up an interesting eyewitness account of the peaks. While searching for the canyon from the air, pilot Jerry Phillips became elated when he finally sighted the elusive twin peaks from a distance. However, he was running short on fuel and had to return to base. When he resumed his search, he couldn't find the elusive peaks a second time. In fact, he never saw them again. Later, in El Paso, Phillips met with Alvin D. Hudson, who claimed to be in possession of a map to the canyon. Hudson told Philips why he never saw the peaks again:

"The reason you could not find your peaks on the return flight is that they do not stand out at all times – they can be seen only at sundown and only on certain days of the year. This is when the sun goes down directly behind them and silhouettes them against a low horizon."[4]

Mackenna's Gold chose to utilize Canyon De Chelly's Speaking Rock/ Spider Rock twin formation for their version of the "twin peaks" signifying the location of Sno-Ta-Hay Canyon. At sunrise, when the dawn light strikes the stone pillars, a strange natural phenomenon occurs, and afterward the shadow of the formation points to the secret door in the film. No such idea is present in any of the legends, though.

Like any lost land, there was also dangerous terrain to cover when reaching the treasure, notably the black-scarred earth of the malpais lava fields. In "The Adams Gold Diggings" by W.H. Byerts, the author gave one of the more grandiose descriptions of the gold hidden in the malpais:

> It would seem as though the Creator, after locating this rich deposit of gold, tried to hide it away for other generations that would follow, for He has covered this part of the country of nearly fifty miles square, with a tremendous flow of lava, and under this lava bed is this treasure house of gold. Now large lava flows or beds in their cooling off, open many in some wide cracks or fissures, and it is at the bottom of one of these large openings lays this gold field. None of the parties tell of the gold being associated with the lava or malpais, but is surrounded by malpais rock, perpendicular walls and only one entrance.

In another grandiose statement, Byerts claimed that "the gold mines of Solomon, the Klondike or Africa may not be compared with [the diggings]." As for the canyon itself, Adams per Byerts said that it was "hemmed in by perpendicular rocks hundreds of feet high as far as we could see in every direction, and our guide told us this canyon was miles long…"

Another vintage depiction of the California Gold Rush.

The perilous canyon walls were exactly why the "secret door" served as Sno-Ta-Hay's lone entrance. An Adams article that appeared in the *St. Louis Globe-Democrat* of February 17, 1889, for instance, told of a failed attempt of prospectors to descend into the canyon by way of an unnamed Navajo man who recounted the incident:

Yes, I know where that mine is. It is very far away; in a canyon that is not like any other. It has no mouth, and is all cliffs, so that you can not [get] into it anywhere, except with very long ropes. The three men found it, and tried to get down into it. The tallest pine tree on the big mountain would not reach down into it. They tied all their lariats together—five lariats. Then one man tied a stick on the end of the rope and sat on it, and the other two began to let him down. Pretty soon a sharp rock in the cliff cut the rope, and he fell to the bottom and was killed.[5]

The Washie Jones account appearing in *Cow Dust and Saddle Leather* gave an interesting description of the canyon as well, mentioning a series of stone steps. (This again brings to mind *Mackenna's Gold*, which featured something similar.) Jones said that the only way of descending into the canyon was down a trail, "which was cut through the rimrock in a series of steps that resembled a stairway."[6]

LOST VALLEY OF THE SCOTCHMAN

In his chapter "The Malpais and Some Maybes" in *Apache Gold & Yaqui Silver*, J. Frank Dobie made a brief mention of a man who allegedly lived near Sno-Ta-Hay Canyon: "They have told of another lost valley [in the malpais] in which a Scotchman used to live distilling whisky that he traded to Indians for nuggets secured nearby, though the Indians would not allow him to take the gold out." [p.115/117.] The Scotchman Dobie spoke of turned out to be Sandy Welch, who arrived in the malpais around 1895. Alfred D. Hudson met Welch in El Paso when he came to his father's store to buy goods with ingots of gold that he had obtained in the malpais. According to the *El Paso Herald* of August 6, 1927, Welch said that "he lived in the roughest part of the malpais with his two dogs as his only companions." Welch claimed that one would never be able to find the place unless they knew where to strike the only trail leading to his shack. Welch frequented a canyon not far from where he lived with a huge gold ledge. Oddly enough, the Apache let him be and even traded with him. However, Welch knew deep down that he could never escape with the gold. On one of his trips to Fort Wingate, Welch asked if some of the soldiers might come to collect him one day at his cabin and escort him out with some of the gold. According to the *Herald*, Welch eventually did just that and retired to parts unknown as a rich man.

In addition to steep cliff walls, the canyon was said to boast a fairly large waterfall. In his pamphlet, "The Adams Diggings Story," Charles Allen claimed that the canyon was "about three hundred yards in width" with "a flat bottom, no trees growing in it, but its sides are covered with pines, rather small, about the right size for log cabins." Allen gave one of the better descriptions of the canyon and its waterfall:

> The spring is on the southwest side of the valley and the water from it floats on the surface for about three miles to a place where the valley narrowed to a box canyon with steep, rocky sides, the box choked with trees, boulders, and rubbish to a depth of about 60 feet, the water flowing over the top of the choke material, forming a waterfall, and sinking into the ground at the base of the falls.

The grandest description of the waterfall came courtesy of an 1897 account published in the *Socorro Chieftain* from R.C. Patterson, who claimed to have gotten the description from Adams himself: "The water in this valley ran northwest and at the lower end fell over a precipice eighty feet high." Any native New Mexican can tell you there are certainly no eighty-foot waterfalls here, and experienced adventurers like Jack Purcell also noted that an eighty-foot waterfall would be unusual in New Mexico and Arizona both.

Another contested detail regarding the canyon's appearance concerned whether an actual placer could be found there. For visual flare, *Mackenna's Gold* made sure to include a striking huge gold vein running through the canyon walls. However, most accounts of the canyon only ever had Adams and his men finding gold nuggets, and very rarely did they ever find a ledge except in offshoots like the one recounted by E.V. Batchler.

Jason Baxter, who allegedly saw Sno-Ta-Hay Canyon for himself in the mid-1870s, was one of the only visitors to the canyon to tell of a streak of quartz. Baxter said, "The water increased as we went up and the canyon walls of white quartz became tinted like a rainbow in the evenin' air. All the clays and rocks looked mineralized."[7]

Another interesting detail to consider was that in most accounts Gotch Ear told the men that an even richer cache of gold could be found nearby. As it was, the miners were so elated with what Gotch Ear showed them, they decided to stay there rather than proceed onto the second, potentially richer site. So, perhaps Baxter explored further up the canyon than Adams and his men did. Or, could it be that Baxter stumbled upon the richer gold site alluded to by Gotch Ear? At this point, we will never know.

Chapter Notes

[1] Some of these attributes are covered in subsequent chapters.
[2] Mckenna, *Black Range Tales*, p.61
[3] Ibid.
[4] Phillips, "A Pilot's Opinion on the Lost Adams," *Gold!*, p.37.
[5] It's important to note that that this canyon was located on a Navajo reservation in this case.
[6] Kemp and Dykes, *Cow Dust and Saddle Leather*, p.268.
[7] McKenna, *Black Range Tales*, p.44.

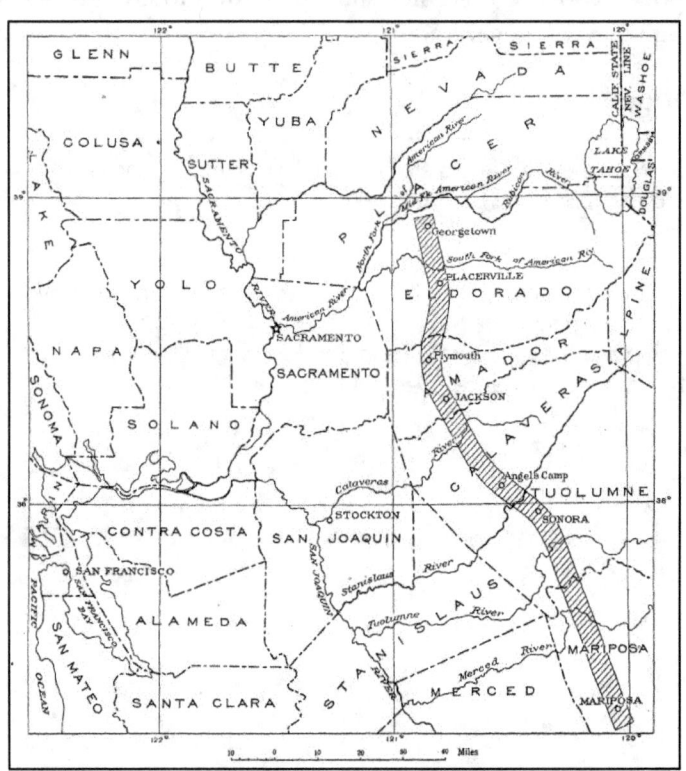

The Mother Lode Belt of California.

6.

THE MOTHER LODE

THE SOURCE OF SNO-TA-HAY CANYON'S GOLD

Almost all of the Adams accounts alluded to an even bigger gold cache waiting to be found elsewhere. For instance, in Byerts' rendition, the Indian guide implied that twenty miles away, very near the two peaks he pointed towards, the miners would find a ledge of gold so rich that a man could "lead any animal away in one day loaded with gold." Likewise, in John Brewer's account, the guide claimed that "There is a little gold in this canyon but not as much as over yonder." *Cow Dust and Saddle Leather* also acknowledged the idea that an even richer placer deposit existed in another canyon nearby, which Adams and his comrades didn't bother to seek out.

It's debatable whether or not anyone ever found this second, richer site, but some Adams hunters have likened it to the "Mother Lode." Colloquially speaking, the Mother Lode refers to the principal placer vein of gold or other precious ore. It has a somewhat mythical quality to it, though a real "mother lode" was found during the California Gold Rush of the 1850s along the Sierra Nevada mountain range.

Similarly, the source of Sno-Ta-Hay Canyon's gold was thought by some to be the Mother Lode of Arizona and New Mexico. A story about a dead prospector found by a group of soldiers on the trail of Geronimo alluded to this in the *Boston*

Sunday Post's article, "A Lost Gold Mine," printed on September 19, 1897. In the article, Ed E. Gosse related how he had been a trooper of the Sixth Cavalry in the spring of 1885. During a campaign in the Mogollon Mountains, he and his troop came across a trail of dead prospectors in search of "the mother lode."

On the forenoon of the third day we came upon the dead body of a prospector, which was hurriedly buried, and we pushed on. About 5 o'clock in the afternoon we found the body of another prospector, killed by the Indians. This man had made a desperate fight in an effort to reach his horse, which was picketed about 100 yards from where he was camped, as shown by the empty shells scattered along the ground.

Gosse continued,

His partner evidently got away some distance, as the Indians left some of their ponies behind for those, who were chasing him to ride when they came back. We had no time to hunt for his partner, and prepared to bury the body we had found. Before burying him the trumpeter of C Troop searched his pockets for papers or letters to identify him. Among other papers were a number of letters from a party in Sliver City, who had evidently been "staking" him and advising him what to do. Among other things he wrote: "Remember, the main object is to discover the mother lode; the diggings may play out, but the mother lode, never."

The idea that the Adams Placer was perhaps the fabled "mother lode" of gold had been put forth before in an earlier article from the *Fort Worth Daily Gazette* of May 10, 1890. The article related that [Adams]

...showed specimens of ore which he had brought out with him and it was the finest ever seen in that locality. It bore evidence of having been picked from a fissure vein, it was free gold-bearing quartz of the finest quality, and samples of it would run hundreds of ounces to the ton. His tale was that he had been prospecting for years, and, like many other miners, believed in a "mother vein," which if found would be of incalculable richness. He followed lead after lead, and all pointed directly to the center of the mountains which ran through the Navajo reservation. At last he became so confident he had the right clew that he determined to brave the dangers of the Indians and go into the reservation to find the 'mother vein.'"

The story said that after "much dodging of Indians," Adams found a pure gold quartz streak in the mountains at a "converging point" of several valleys. "The pure white of the quartz was crossed with free gold in countless directions, and it looked as if it need only to be crushed for the precious metal to flow out." Adams procured a few specimens before the Navajo came along and escorted him off the reservation with what little gold he was able to hide on his person.

It's an odd rendition of the tale for sure, and ended with Adams dying, but not in the canyon. Instead, this Adams was reported to have been found dead in his cabin, the theory being that he had been strangled in his sleep. As Adams had been organizing a company to go with him to mine the mother lode, it was thought that one of the members killed him, thinking they knew everything they needed to know and could get to the main vein without him. The murderer was never caught, and presumably no one found the gold either.

While the above story was just another of the numerous retellings of the Adams legend, is it possible that the nuggets found by the real Adams and his men came from the Mother Lode of the Southwest? Perhaps.

Chief Nana, also called Nanay, in his later years.

7.

GHOST OF CHIEF NANA
TALES OF APACHE SENTRIES

Among the pantheon of great Apache chiefs, Chief Nana is often overlooked when compared to the likes of Victorio and Mangas Coloradas. (Geronimo was technically never given the rank of chief, by the way.) However, Nana was one of the most powerful and unique chiefs of the Apache for many reasons. Born in 1810, he was in his sixties by the time of the tumultuous Victorio War raids of the late 1870s. After the younger chief perished in 1880, Nana took over for Victorio. Like Geronimo, Nana eventually surrendered in 1886 and became confined to the reservations.

Partly to thank for Nana's longevity was the possession of a supernatural quantity known to the Apache as "Power," an invisible life force which flowed through all things. To harness the Power, the Apache had to endure a four-day fast in the wilderness. Power often pertained to the abilities of premonition and healing, though Geronimo was even said to be able to control the weather at times. Nana had Power over rattlesnakes and in securing ammunition. Ace Daklugie, son of Juh and nephew of Geronimo, said when younger men tried and failed to secure ammunition, that "when Nana, long past eighty and crippled, rode all night, he brought back ammunition."[1]

Though a few odd accounts erroneously swapped Nana for Geronimo, Nana was the chief most associated with the Adams Diggings. Almost all accounts agreed that it was he who spoke with the miners. Besides that, there were several other sources linking Nana with the gold. After surrendering in 1886, Nana befriended an Indian trader, James Chase, at the Warm Springs Apache Agency. According to Chase, Nana actually told him about the Adams Diggings. Chase asked how far away they were and Nana responded, "two days for a white man, one day for an Indian." When Chase asked where they were, Nana gestured to the northwest. Also lining up with other accounts, when Chase asked the name of the place, Nana responded that it was Sno-Ta-Hay.

Warm Springs Apache Agency c. 1901.

Yet another link to Nana and the gold came via Niño Cochise, grandson of the famous chief and nephew of Geronimo. In 1927, at the age of ninety-eight, Niño dictated his life story to A. Kenny Griffith and had it published as *The First Hundred Years of Nino Cochise (The Untold Story of an Apache Indian Chief)*. The tome included a few surprising details pertaining to the Lost Adams. In the book, Niño mentioned how "After about a week of resting, feasting, boasting, and getting roaring drunk, Nanay took a small group and worked in Sno-Ta-Hay, our gold mine just a few kilometers from camp."[2] Later, he mentioned it again, claiming, "We reopened our gold mine; this was the Spanish gold vein Nanay had discovered years before, and the Wild Ones had worked at times. Now that they were gone, we worked it, calling it Sno-Ta-Hay 'just lying there.'"[3]

Needless to say, these two tales of Nana working the gold mine or offering to show it to White Eyes were quite at odds with reports that placed

Niño Cochise on postcard.

Nana as the chief guardian of the canyon. As to why Nana so fiercely guarded the canyon, in his paper, "Nana's Gold," Austin T. King wrote that Sno-Ta-Hay Canyon "was part of his spirit, his religion, his Mother Earth."[4] In the same article, Austin even implied that Nana might've been the one who hid the canyon in later years, writing, "It is likely that either an earth slide covered it or Nana diverted the stream on the first level to conceal the canyon." Austin concluded his article by stating, "Nana's spirit stands guard over the famous canyon, like Cheetwach's spirit guards the Lost Padre Mine... Nana's gold will remain hidden for some time, you can be sure."[5]

And indeed, for many years it was said that spectral sentinels guarded the canyon. In fact, they haunted men's dreams before they could even arrive in some instances. In *Black Range Tales*, James McKenna related the night that Jason Baxter told his rendition of the Lost Adams Diggings that their cook, "Swedish Nelson," was anticipating the tale so much that he had had a nightmare about the diggings. Interestingly, it was evocative of a modern zombie movie, as Nelson claimed that

Apaches rose out of the ground, or as he put it, came "poppin' up out'n the ground like corn from a skillet."[6] The Apaches wore belts about their waists with the scalps of their victims as well as a "long string o' human ears and fingers around his neck instead of beads."[7]

SAN CARLOS APACHES, ARIZONA

One man who was able to attest to the appearance of living Apache guardians in the canyon was James B. Gray, who had been chief of scouts for the San Carlos Indian reservation. In his later years, Gray spoke with J. Frank Dobie, and Gray's wife also wrote about his experience for *New Mexico Magazine*. Gray said that during his time as chief of scouts for the San Carlos reservation, he could often sense the presence of Indian sentinels watching him in the mountains.

For what it's worth, Gray's testimony did seem to suggest that he found Sno-Ta-Hay Canyon and went there several times. However, he apparently traveled there one time too many. On one of his return visits, eight Apache snuck up on him and tied him to a tree. Gray assumed the Apache were about to either torture him or kill him when, luckily, a medicine man named Go-sho-nay appeared. Go-sho-nay, whom Gray had befriended on the reservation, ordered his companions to release Gray as long as he would promise never to return to the canyon. Go-sho-nay informed Gray that the canyon was sacred to his people, and they watched it day and night in all seasons.

Apache ghosts being called upon to act as guardians was not unheard of. Nana claimed to have seen a medicine man summon the ghosts of Cochise, Victorio, and Mangas Coloradas, who rose up from the earth before sinking back into the ground in June of 1881. The medicine man was a Coyotero Apache called Nock-ay-det-klinne, who was also rumored to hunt down prospectors with golden bullets. Nock-ay-det-klinne was killed during the Battle of Cibecue Creek later that same year in August of 1881. (Pictured above are Geronimo, far right, and three of his warriors in 1886.)

Chiricahua prisoners of war, including Geronimo, third from right in the front row, in 1886. Lozen, the fierce female warrior and sister of Victorio, is thought to be among the women in this photo. Like Geronimo, Lozen was adept at the usage of Power, in her case being able to locate enemies from long distances.

In his book the *Lost Canyon of Gold*, W.C. Jameson also mentioned these sentinels, writing, "They have been spotted against the backdrop of the sky along the ridges, sometimes unmoving, sometimes disappearing only to reappear at another location."[8] As opposed to flesh and blood human beings, could these have been ghostly guardians? One thing is for certain; whether real or spectral, sentinels by all accounts stand guard over the canyon, and the spirit of Nana lives on.

Chapter Notes

---

[1] Ball, *Indeh*, p.62.

[2] Cochise, *First Hundred Years*, p.6. (There's a possibility worth noting that the Apache may have referred to any gold nuggets found above ground as *Sno-Ta-Hay*, "just lying there." As such, it's possible there may have been a few "Sno-Ta-Hay Canyons" for the Apache and that the "mine" Niño Cochise spoke of was not the Lost Adams Diggings.)

[3] Ibid, p.29.

[4] This comes from a photocopied paper found in the archives of the Historical Society for Southeast New Mexico. Unfortunately, it bore no date or source, simply the author and the title.

[5] King, "Nana's Gold."

[6] McKenna, *Black Range Tales*, p.33.

[7] Ibid. The following night around the campfire, when Baxter proceeded to tell them the next portion of the ordeal, Nelson revealed he had had yet another nightmare about the diggings. In this case, he said that as he was harvesting his golden nuggets, rather than Apaches, he saw a silver tip grizzly bear as big as an elephant. Though Nelson made no connection, it may have been no coincidence that the Apache greatly revered the bear, thinking it to be either a witch in the form of an animal or an Apache who had been reincarnated as a bear as some form of penance.

[8] Jameson, *Lost Canyon of Gold*, p.xvii.

8.

ADAM'S GOLD

ADAMS GOES AT IT ALONE

The reporters working on behalf of the Federal Writer's Project in the 1930s dug up some real whoppers on the diggings every so often. Actually, this one doesn't really qualify as a "whopper" so much as an odd variation of the Adams legend. "The Story of Adam's Diggings" by L. Raines changed Adams to Adam, thus making it Adam's Diggings:

> This story was given to me by Duane Aul, son of a rancher, who has lived near the scenes of the events which he narrates. He has retold the story as he has heard it many times around the fireside on winter evenings.
>
> Many years before New Mexico became a state, Adam and his partner worked a mine in the Zuni Mountains. As soon as the men had mined a few hundred pounds of gold, they loaded it on donkeys and started south to trade for supplies. The trail that they followed led from San Rafael, a village a few miles west of Grants, New Mexico, to Gold Spring, where they always camped. Covering a distance of several miles, they passed the next night in the home of an old Spanish woman at Tinaja. When they left Tinaja no one knew the destination except that the trail led south to some city perhaps below the border. The trip usually took at least two months.

Zuni Mountains of New Mexico c.1908.

After one of these southern trips, which he had made alone, Adam failed to return. His partner went in search of him but found no trace of him in the south. When he tried to return to the mine he could not find the trail. He settled in the Tinaja Valley, but after about twenty years' meager existence on the income from the ranch he decided to make one more effort to find the mine. Accompanied by a friend, he searched for weeks and at last was rewarded by finding an old trail sign. With the hope of regained wealth once more stirring in his mind he camped at the old sign just five miles from the mine. He told his friend that he was sure that he could lead him to the mine the next morning, for he recalled clearly that the trail led to a crevice in the rocks and down the crevice to a box canyon and in the canyon was the mine. During the night he became ill and died.

Since that time several parties have searched for the mine and the rumor is that there is a well marked map of the trail in existence. One party reported that it found a box canyon into which it descended with ropes over 100 foot ledge. On the bottom of the canyon were found a copper kettle, a pic, a shovel, and other articles. No trace of gold has ever been found.

Obviously, this story was merely the result of an old-timer misremembering the tale of Adams and perhaps conjoining it with an unrelated find. And, though they are certainly within the confines of what one might call "Lost Adams Country," the Zuni Mountains are a bit too far north to be a real contender for the location of the diggings.

Ruins near Fort Wingate.

9.

LOST CITY of the LOST ADAMS
CLIFF DWELLINGS IN THE CANYON

One of the more fantastic aspects of *Mackenna's Gold* was the addition of cliff-dwelling ruins in the canyon. They served no real purpose in the story other than providing some striking imagery and puzzled many Adams enthusiasts. This is primarily because J. Frank Dobie only gave the ruins a passing mention in *Apache Gold & Yaqui Silver*. In a blink and you'll miss it line, Dobie wrote that certain Lost Adams hunters had "been responsible for a widely believed description of ancient cliff-dwellings hanging on the walls of a watered valley glimpsed accidentally by two or three white men, always unable to return to it."[1]

Dobie apparently either didn't find enough on the cliff dwellings to elaborate upon or perhaps didn't feel that they fit his story. Alvin D. Hudson, a Texas-based turquoise dealer, gave an in-depth account of the ancient ruins in the *El Paso Herald*. Hudson had a friend who was a Pueblo Indian whose father had been an Indian scout in the days of the campaign against Geronimo during the 1870s and early 1880s. The *Herald* of August 6, 1927, stated, "When Hudson's friend was only a boy his father used to tell him of a wonderful lost city he had seen on one of his scouting expeditions."[2]

The article continued that the scout had just endured an arduous trek across the malpais when he came upon "the north bank of a deep box canyon just after sunset."[3]

THESE photos were taken on a trip A. D. Hudson, C. B. Wilson, A. F. Wilson and O. A. Aultman made into New Mexico. They were snapped near the Malpais, where the lost diggin's are said to be located.

Photo printed in the *El Paso Herald* of August 6, 1927, showing one of Hudson's expeditions in search of the Lost Adams in the malpais.

The scout camped there for the night and saw the "lost city" the next morning just before sunrise:

> He was looking down into the canyon when on one of the canyon walls he saw a large group of cliff dwellings under a protecting cliff. Even as he watched the sun began to rise and as the long shadows shot across the canyon and blotted out the city before his very eyes."
>
> Evidently the only time the city could be seen from any distance was just before sunrise, the old scout said.[4]

The old government scout made a subsequent trip into the malpais again thirty years later and returned home with gold nuggets and pieces of turquoise. Just before he died in 1896, he told his son he had found the gold in the same canyon as the lost city.

Hudson was fascinated by the tale because he felt that the "lost city" was either located within Sno-Ta-Hay Canyon or nearby. Hudson also had an archeologist friend, C.B. Wilson of El Paso, who was taken to the city by an Indian guide in 1918. Initially, Wilson was told by another Indian friend that if he wanted to "see something that few white men had ever seen" there was a man at Laguna Pueblo who could take him to a "lost city." The Laguna man, so Wilson was told, had been following a wounded deer one day when he suddenly found himself in front of a wonderful city akin to an old Spanish mission. A solid gold bell hung from its tower, and inside the mission, images of hammered gold were on the altar—or so the guide said.

Unfortunately, no detailed accounts exist of the cliff dwellings alleged to exist among the Adams Diggings, but they likely resemble Montezuma Castle of Arizona, pictured above (c.1897 by Edgar A. Mearns). It's also worth noting that the idea of cliff dwellings within the canyon visible only at certain times of day is similar to the legend of the "White Pueblo of the Malpais." According to myth, it can only be glimpsed during the setting rays of the sun, its white form standing out amidst the black lava flow. Could the real account of the cliff dwellings only visible in the morning light be related in some way to the fable?

Eventually, Wilson took the unnamed Laguna man up on his offer. Over the course of four days, Wilson was led through the treacherous malpais to the canyon. Rather than using the secret door (assuming that it was actually Sno-Ta-Hay Canyon), Wilson and his guide approached via the north rim of the canyon wall and descended by rope. The descent took up the better part of a day, and was made a bit more cumbersome due to Wilson taking along a camera. This wasn't at Wilson's insistence though, but rather the guide's. The guide, well aware of the sentinels of Sno-Ta-Hay, insisted that Wilson "carry [the camera] as prominently as possible" in an effort to show that his interest was purely academic and that he was not a prospector after gold. The *Herald* explained that down in the canyon, "Obviously believing that they were being watched, the guide by talking loudly and with gesticulations made it plain to anyone who might have been hiding in the canyon that they were interested in ruins and not gold."[5]

This map published in the *El Paso Herald* on August 13, 1927, placed the diggings in the vicinity of Laguna Pueblo.

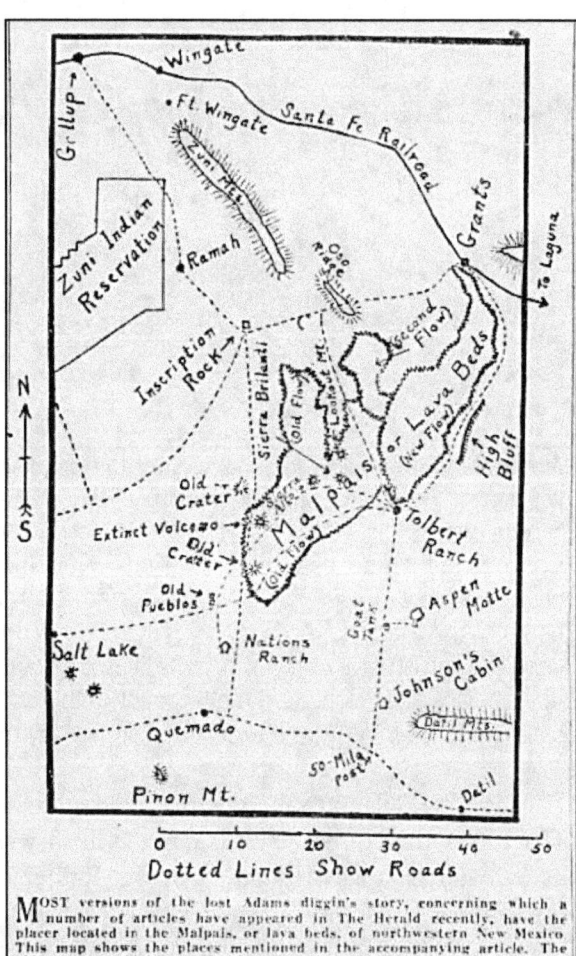

Dotted Lines Show Roads

MOST versions of the lost Adams diggin's story, concerning which a number of articles have appeared in The Herald recently, have the placer located in the Malpais, or lava beds, of northwestern New Mexico. This map shows the places mentioned in the accompanying article. The old prospector, Johnson, mentioned in the story, believes the diggin's are located near Laguna, several miles to the east of the northern part of the lava beds.

3053
Cliff Dwellings
Gila River,
Silver City,
N. Mex.

The Gila Cliff Dwellings are in what could be considered the general area of the Adams Diggings. In fact, during their trek to Sno-Ta-Hay Canyon, Jason Baxter and James McKenna stopped at the ruins to explore. While there, they found small, mummified human remains. Though often explained as the bodies of children, small, mummified corpses possessing adult teeth have been found in cliff dwellings elsewhere, notably at Montezuma Castle in Arizona and in the San Pedro Mountains of Wyoming (inset). Believers in the paranormal think these small mummies might be the "little people" spoken of by many indigenous tribes. Eve Ball even came across honest witness testimonies of them in her interviews. Eugene Chihuahua told her that high up on a mountain where Juh lived he saw one, which he at first mistook for another child. However, when he got closer, he saw that it was a full-grown man only a few feet high. Ace Daklugie later explained to Chihuahua that the little people lived in the forest and were "just small people who never die. And they mean good to the Apaches."[6] Is it possible that McKenna and Baxter found the remains of one of these little people? "The most interesting thing we found was a perfect mummy with cottonwood fiber woven around it. The length of the figure was about 18 inches," McKenna remembered. "Their small size, the small handprints on the wall, and the small openings between rooms it seems to tell of a race of short people; however, skeletons found in other ruins do not bear out this idea." McKenna related one other interesting nugget of information, stating, "The Apaches never used these caves, saying they had belonged to a people who lived in the Gila country years before they came there."[7] Could it be the Apache stayed away due to reverence of the magical little people? And, if there really were cliff dwellings in Sno-Ta-Hay Canyon, could they too have been inhabited by little people and have been another reason the canyon was sacred?

Though Wilson and the guide were honestly there in the interest of seeing the ruins, that didn't stop the guide from showing Wilson the gold. "Talking in low asides to my friend while pointing to interesting scenes, the guide called his attention at one place in the canyon to some loose ore," the *Herald* reported. "Have you ever seen gold?" the guide asked his companion in a low voice, then immediately added in a shout, "That tree over there would make a good picture." [8]

More ancient ruins in the vicinity of Fort Wingate.

"There are three nuggets by your feet. Don't look down suddenly but pick them up in a minute and in a casual way," the guide whispered, then "carelessly picked up a handful of gravel and began flipping the pieces this way and that as he gestured and pointed." Wilson did as told and "managed to conceal a couple of the nuggets in his hand without arousing the suspicion of any possible watchers." [9]

After looking at the cliff dwellings from a distance and kicking around the canyon for a bit, "the two made their way out by the south entrance," perhaps meaning the zigzag route so often spoken of, and in a day and a half, arrived at the place where they had left their automobile.

So, perhaps *Mackenna's Gold* wasn't as far off as it initially appeared by including cliff dwellings in the canyon? Furthermore, there are numerous cliff dwellings in the area, most notably the Gila Cliff Dwellings. As such, it's not terribly far-fetched to think that ancient ruins may reside within Sno-Ta-Hay Canyon, even though it certainly is a romantic notion.

Chapter Notes

[1] Dobie, *Apache Gold & Yaqui Silver*, p.115.

[2] "EL PASOAN HAS OLD MAP TO MUCH SOUGHT PLACER," *El Paso Herald* (August 6, 1927).

[3] Ibid.

[4] Ibid.

[5] "EL PASOAN PLANS SEARCH FOR LOST ADAMS DIGGIN'S," *El Paso Herald* (July 16, 1927).

[6] Robinson, *Apache Voices*, p.184.

[7] McKenna, *Black Range Tales*, p.50.

[8]"EL PASOAN PLANS SEARCH FOR LOST ADAMS DIGGIN'S," *El Paso Herald* (July 16, 1927).

[9] Ibid.

Henry "Walkalong" Smith (right) with Kenneth Elijah Bain along Collingsworth Road in El Paso, Texas, c. 1937. (Palace of the Governor's Photo Archives, #105059)

10.

WALKALONG SMITH

BILLY THE KID & THE LOST ADAMS

Over the years, the Adams Diggings have been prone to some strange bedfellows—chief among them Billy the Kid. Actually, that Billy the Kid might have some connections to Adams isn't too odd since both men wandered the West, specifically Arizona and New Mexico, throughout the 1870s. Heck, considering Billy the Kid's mother, Katherine Antrim, operated a boarding house in Silver City in the early 1870s, it's even possible that Adams may have been a guest there once.

While that's interesting to ponder, folklore and hearsay of the old-timers provided a more fantastic link to that of Adams and the Kid—that being that the Kid found the Adams Diggings! Like the men who claimed to be a surviving Jesse James, there were many claimants to the Boy Bandit King's throne after he bit the dust. The best-known of these was undoubtedly Brushy Bill Roberts of Hico, Texas, with John Miller of Ramah, New Mexico, in close second. And then there was Henry "Walkalong" Smith.[1]

Actually, Smith never claimed to be the Kid; others did that for him after he was conveniently dead and could no longer speak. Perhaps this was because Smith seemed to be incredibly knowledgeable on the Kid, often telling stories about him. Among those tales was one where Billy escaped Garrett's gun in Fort Sumner on July 14, 1881.

The typical account of the Kid's death had him going outside to cut a piece from a side of beef hanging on the porch when he noticed that his host, Pete Maxwell, had a guest in his bedroom. Billy walked in to see who it was; the guest was Garrett, and he shot the Kid dead. According to Smith, Billy never ventured out to cut any beef the night of July 14, and sent one of the Maxwell servants to do so and they caught Garrett's bullet instead. Billy hid out in one of Maxwell's spare rooms as word spread that he had been killed. Seizing the opportunity, the Kid and his friends decided to seal the deal of his death in an act of fakery. A hasty coffin was fashioned, the body of the servant boy was hidden, and Billy then played dead in the coffin for the Coroner's Jury. This wild story was told by Smith to John Graham in Reserve, New Mexico, which could likely be what later led other old-timers to label Smith himself as Billy the Kid.

THE FINALE—THE KID KILLED BY THE SHERIFF AT FORT SUMNER. Page 128.

Illustration depicting the death of Billy the Kid.

Walkalong Smith, also known as "Fiddling" Henry Smith, was a wanderer of New Mexico who walked everywhere he went. Smith would often stay at secluded ranches where he would earn his keep by teaching the rancher's children reading, writing, and sometimes music before he would mysteriously disappear.[2] Smith never stayed in one place for long. The only things he carried with him on his long journeys were a few books, some pencils, and a weather-beaten writing tablet. He was also frequently seen browsing through the archives of the Governor's Palace in Santa Fe.

When Smith was found dead outside of Lordsburg in 1937, the truth of this enigmatic figure was finally "revealed" by the ranchers who had known him best. Henry Smith had really been Billy the Kid. According to the ranchers, during the aftermath of the Lincoln County War, Billy had captured the sympathy of Governor Lew Wallace. During a secret meeting, Pat Garrett and Governor Wallace had decided that the Kid was innocent for his crimes committed during the war and that he had only killed in vengeance and self-defense. Governor Wallace was still powerless to protect the Kid from the mighty Santa Fe Ring, and so it was decided a shootout would be staged in Ft. Sumner to fake the Kid's death, at which point two bags of sand would be buried in an empty coffin and the Kid sent off to a prestigious university in secrecy.[3]

If the story is true, the Kid returned to New Mexico twenty years later at the turn of the century under the guise of Walkalong Smith. But there's more. As if Smith's secret identity wasn't fantastic enough, he was also a treasure hunter searching for the Lost Adams Diggings. During his wanderings, Smith collected every bit of information he could on the diggings. More specifically, though, Smith was making a thorough list of all the men who had been killed in search of Adams' gold. If Smith ever did find the diggings, people said he was doing it for the good of the state and would deliver the wealth from the gold to charity.

While Smith may well have been a searcher for the Lost Adams Diggings, he most likely was not a reformed Billy the Kid. Though it's true the two men did share a few similarities, such as a penchant for music and dance as well as befriending and staying at the homes of ranchers, Smith was said to never touch a gun, not even to kill a rattlesnake. Of course, some said this was because Smith had let go of his wild gun fighting days to lead a more serene life. Journalist Will Robinson, wrote of Walkalong Smith in the late 1930s, saying, "Frank Dobie tied [Billy the Kid] up with 'Silent Smith,' the mystery school teacher in the Deming terrain, this though [sic] Billy could read and write."

Actually, prior to his time in the Deming region, Smith frequented Billy's old haunt of Lincoln. In 1900, Smith taught school in Lincoln, as remembered by Laurie Bastion, one of his ten-year-old students at the time. She described Smith as a stuffy, refined man who spoke in perfect English, never in slang. He was known to have remarked that he preferred being a teacher to going to jail—whatever that meant. Years later, in 1916, Laurie was married with children of her own and living in Socorro. Smith had moved there, too, and had been teaching at the School of Mines. Assuming the whole Billy the Kid searching out the Lost Adams conspiracy theory was just that, it's likely that Smith learned of and became fascinated with the diggings during his time in Catron County. There, he walked back and forth between Datil and Magdalena and across the San Augustin Plains. Laurie noticed that on his person, he kept a detailed journal devoted to the diggings, plus a few novels he had written and hoped to see published.[4]

Illustration of the New Mexico School of Mines c.1894.

According to Dobie, Smith expired late in 1937 while crawling towards a mountain, presumably to find a cave to die in. However, there is evidence that Dobie got his dates wrong and that Smith didn't die until later. It also seems to be too much of a coincidence that another Kid claimant, John Miller, died in November of 1937. Adding to the confusion, an article in *The El Paso Times* on July 26, 1964, mentioned a retired

Immigration officer named Leslie Traylor, who claimed that Billy the Kid was really Henry "Street" Smith, who was buried in the Arizona Pioneer Home under the name of John Miller.

As it turns out, the Lincoln County Heritage Trust obtained an obituary of 98-year-old Henry "Street" Smith, who did in fact die in the Pioneers Home, albeit on October 17, 1955, not 1937.[5] (For those now wondering if this was a different Henry Smith, he was not, for his obituary photo showed the same man in the two confirmed pictures of Walkalong Smith belonging to the LCHT.)

"Billy the Kid" Died Oct. 17 1955

The Arizona Republic, Phoenix, Arizona

Arizona Deaths

Henry Street Smith, 97, Dies At Pioneers Home

PRESCOTT—Henry Street Smith, 97, the oldest male guest at the Pioneers Home here, died here yesterday. He would have reached 98 in three weeks.

Mr. Smith was born in Glasgow, Ky. Dennison, a station non the railroad six miles southeast of Parker, was his first stop in Arizona, in 1880 with army troops.

After his college education in the East, Mr. Smith returned to Arizona, and became one of the early-day school teachers. He helped survey the line between Arizona and New Mexico.

A bachelor, he is survived by two nephews, Moulton B. Smith, Phoenix, and Sumner M. Smith, with the armed services.

Funeral services will be conducted at 10 a.m. tomorrow at the Ruffner Funeral Home in Prescott.

Minnie Mae Durham

PIONEER DIES — Henry Street Smith, 97, oldest male guest at the Pioneers Home in Prescott, died yesterday. Born in Kentucky, he came to the state in 1880.

Smith's obituary, printed on October 17, 1955.

Smith was listed as being born in Kentucky and came to New Mexico in 1880. There he worked as an early day schoolteacher and also "helped survey the line between New Mexico and Arizona." As such, one might assume that Dobie heard of Billy the Kid claimant John Miller's passing in 1937, and somehow mixed this up with a false story of Smith (who would have been in his seventies) dropping dead outside Deming.[6]

Whatever the case, any story that can combine Billy the Kid, the Lost Adams Diggings, and an elaborate 1881 government conspiracy is certainly an interesting one.

Chapter Notes

[1] He was also referred to as "Walkabout" Smith and "Street" Smith.

[2] Among those given lessons were *True West* editor Bob Boze Bell's aunt in the Deming area.

[3] An even more fantastic flourish added that the Kid went through whatever the 1880s equivalent of reconstructive surgery was to conceal his identity.

[4] In *Die Rich Here!*, author Ralph Reynolds noted that Smith showed Laurie Bastion's husband one of his novels. Not surprisingly, it was a Western, though Mr. Bastion felt it lacked enough violence, which Smith resented.

[5] Actually, Smith's age lined up pretty closely with the age the real Billy the Kid would have been in 1955, considering he was born in 1859.

[6] Likewise, Leslie Taylor probably was aware of Dobie's Walkalong Smith story and John Miller's passing. When Smith, being "Billy the Kid" in her mind, passed away in 1955, she may have become confused enough to think that Henry Smith was buried as John Miller.

11.

THE LOST TEXAS DIGGINS
QUITMAN MOUNTAINS GOLD

Ever hear the one about the old prospector who found a lost canyon of gold, survived an Apache raid, went to California, then periodically returned to the southwest to search for his lost gold only to never find it? Well, you're about to hear it again—and it ain't Adams. However, the story is so uncannily similar you would be hard-pressed not to think it was a carbon copy of the Lost Adams legend, only set in Texas. The account ran in the *El Paso Herald* of August 3, 1912, which it should be noted was prior to the paper running their popular series on the Lost Adams.

In the article, an ex-El Paso County surveyor named A.H. Parker told of hearing the story from a prospector named W.W. Williams about twenty years before. Williams was in Parker's office due to the fact that in 1883, Texas had just passed some new mining laws. Williams told Parker how in 1875 he had accidentally discovered some "gold diggings" while he was running lines for a railroad company with a party of surveyors. Williams told of traveling ten miles northeast from Fort Quitman into the Quitman Mountains. Along with the surveyors were some Ysleta Indians, who informed the surveyors that there was a spring in a nearby canyon.

Going into the canyon to get water, they soon discovered gold nuggets amidst the sand and gravel in the gulch and began panning for gold. Though some of it was quite coarse, the surveyors became quite excited. Knowing that the gold had been caused by the erosion of veins in the mountains, Williams set out to find the main vein. "I determined to prospect a little in the higher places for some vein," Williams said. "Finally my search was rewarded. On a ridge some distance up I found a vein of quartz which was very rich in native gold."[1] Williams broke off some samples, wrapped them in a handkerchief, and then "placed a couple of mounds of rock to mark the place."[2]

Coincidentally, the landmarks Williams associated with the area comprised of "two pyramidal, whitish gray peaks, which are called Sierra Blanca peaks." If you'll recall, some of the main landmarks in the tale of Adams were two peaks near the canyon. As it turned out, this was only one of several other coincidences with the Adam story, for next up came the band of marauding Apaches. Specifically, the Ysleta Indian guides spotted some Apache while they were out hunting and believed they were coming to camp at the spring. As such, Williams and his fellow surveyors fled the spring under the cover of darkness and traveled all night until they came to Eagle Springs.

Postcard of Interstate Highway 10 with the Quitman Mountains in the background.

Like Adams, upon returning to civilization, Williams showed his gold samples around San Antonio, where he eventually garnered the interest of fellow treasure hunters to make a return trip.[3] However, upon entering the Quitman Mountains

The author of the article did his homework and managed to dig up a corroborating story, perhaps proving this wasn't actually inspired by the Adams Diggings and really was just a similar story. The other incident occurred in the 1860s and had a man named John Ryland trying to access Eagle Springs by means of an alternate route through which he accidentally stumbled across the same spring that Williams camped at. Along the river, he found several pieces of rich quartz gold, which he took back with him to San Antonio. Using the gold in San Antonio, he attracted investors to return with them to the area. Shades of Gotch Ear, Ryland told his fellow prospectors that if he failed to lead them to the gold that they could hang him on the spot. However, unlike Gotch Ear, he did not find the gold though his party was nice enough not to hang him. Instead, Ryland was flogged and driven out of camp in the direction of El Paso never to be seen again.

with the new party, they were attacked by a band of Indians.[4] Though two of the party perished, the rest escaped with their lives. This experience naturally made Williams hesitant about returning.

That brought Parker up to speed and Williams told him:

> "After all these years… I have come back to revisit the scene of my discovery. In all my experiences I have never seen a ledge so rich in gold as the one I found at that time. I know I can go right to the place, and when I have located some claims I shall return to see you with the proof."[5]

A few weeks later, Williams returned, and, like Adams, came back empty-handed. He told Parker that he had found "what he supposed to be the very place," but that "the spring had either dried up or been buried, and although the ridge and other landmarks looked familiar, still he had been unable to find the vein."[6] Williams searched through other canyons in the area, but all seemed to look alike to him. "The more he looked around the more he became bewildered and mystified," the article said.

Like Adams, "Williams soon realized he was another victim of the elusive lure of the hills of gold, and was simply adding another chapter to the stories of lost gold mines."[7] Eventually,

Williams found himself in an old soldiers' home in California, but periodically came back to Texas throughout the 1890s and the early 1900s in search of the gold, much like old man Adams before him in New Mexico and Arizona.

Chapter Notes

[1] "Lost Gold Mines in the Quitman Mountains, and Stories About Them," *El Paso Herald* (August 3, 1912).

[2] Ibid.

[3] As for one final bizarre attribute, the article speculated that the gold may have been of Aztec origin. The article reported that in the mountains was found a jar "with strange Aztec hieroglyphics engraved on one side," and how in the same vicinity was discovered gold along with "a fragment of an old stone arrastra, or gold mill."

[4] In another odd coincidence, the story also featured an Apache maiden named Nana, who told her "cowboy sweetheart" that "her people used to gather placer gold in a canyon of the Quitmans even when construction work was in progress on the railroads."

[5] "Lost Gold Mines in the Quitman Mountains, and Stories About Them," *El Paso Herald* (August 3, 1912).

[6] Ibid.

[7] Ibid.

12.

FOOLS GOLD

A POT OF GOLD IN A RING OF ROSES

The idea that Old Man Adams was nothing but a liar has been bandied about many times. However, the following account proposed that the whole affair was nothing but a mescal-induced practical joke that went too far. Via the *Copper Era and Morenci Leader* of December 31, 1903, a contributor identified only by their initials, J.H.V., gave a lengthy and wild variation of the Adams legend.

J.H.V. said little of himself in the letter, but implied that he was an elderly man who used to be an Indian trader at San Pedro prior to the Civil War. He spoke of friendship with the White Mountain Apache that he traded with, and stated that some of them used gold nuggets as currency. As such, he tried to entice the Apache to show him the main placer. Just when he felt he was getting close to winning their confidence, the Civil War broke out and he left to join the fight.

It was after the war that J.H.V. heard the varying versions of the Adams legend, and the account that he was given took place prior to the Civil War. J.H.V. stated that in 1858, in the aftermath of the Gadson Treaty, a group of surveyors was sent to map the area of the Gila and San Francisco Rivers in Arizona. Along the way, they met a party from Sonora that joined their numbers with "new made mescal," or liquor. Two of the men, and it's not clear which party they were originally a part of, were identified as Adams and Blair. The duo overslept on the wrong side of the Gila River, resulting in the following:

> The river rose and they were left and it seems forgotten until some weeks after some U.S. dragoons from Fort Bucannon out on a hunt found them in a very hard fix and took them back with them to the fort. When there they told a tale of their wanderings, saying they had found a gulch in which wild roses grew and a big placer mine and had their tobacco sacks full of nuggets of dark colored gold which they had picked up. No inducement would make them go back nor would they part with the nuggets, but they had them for they were seen and hefted by many.

Postcard of the San Francisco River in Clifton, Arizona c.1920.

The tale resumed in 1869, with J.H.V. relating that in "1869 in Tucson came to the store ... at Camp Lowell... a lone, sandy complectioned [sic] man who said his name was Adams" who "told in substance the same story of the Adams Diggings which is current today." In other words, the man did not relate the modest tale of the two lost surveyors who found gold near the Gila River. He related the whole Adams shebang, Apache attack and all. In the store that day was a listener identified only as Captain Hines, who suspected the tale was a gross exaggeration based upon the more down-to-earth tale of the surveyors. Not only that, but Captain Hines, "who was then a government contractor an ex-captain in the California volunteers," recognized the man "as having served in his company under the name of Edwards" rather than Adams.

Fort Yuma on the Colorado River.

Captain Hines' lengthy dismantling of "Adams" account, though somewhat poorly written, is worth reprinting:

> You say that in 1858 just eleven years ago, you crossed the Colorado river at Yuma, never went to the trading post and stage station, but to a camp of Yuma Indians to enquire the way up the river, when there was a road in which a daily stage was running. In this camp you found a Mexican captive, whom you [purchased] that he might show you this gold mine. He then held a share. All this in sight of Fort Yuma, over which old glory was flying. You trailed up the Gila to the Maricopas… When there you struck the stage road, why did you not go to the station and trading post? Americans were there. Were you not getting about out of tobacco by this time? You say you followed the Gila and crossed into New Mexico, why, my man, you were there after you crossed the Colorado in 1858. The first shake out of the box your

slave and two others were killed, but you never stopped to bury them, but pressed on, and sure enough you had struck it! You say you then located claims. Now where did you expect to put them on record? You built, so you say, cabins too, with fireplaces. Now tell us, did you turn the arch or did you hunt a big rock? You cut channels to bedrock to ground sluice. Now what I want to know is this, (the captain had been a blacksmith in his young days), how did you sharpen all those tools? You soon cleaned up $200,000 in gold, and your grub was getting short and you had lost all your stock, so twelve men loaded up this 400 pound weight of gold and their grub and started back for Yuma, over 250 miles away, it looks strange that men who had the means to fit out a party such as you describe did not know that to the southeast you were some 100 miles from La Mesilla, where there were stores, a grist mill and a newspaper, but they started for Yuma, and then you washed out another 400 pound pot of gold, and then you and one other lucky man started out. Right then your camp was jumped and cleaned out, and the same moon you walked on the bleaching bones of your twelve old pards. The gold was gone but there they lay just as they fell. You fellows must have been living on chili straight for some time or the coyotes would surely have carried them around, but you got to the Gila all right and the next you know you were at Franklin, Texas. Now, there were a lot of good men there who would have helped you bring in all that gold…
You went back to California the year before the war, you say, with an immigrant train passed on foot in sight, of the mountains in which you built a cabin with a fire place, while the Indians were shooting at you and under the hearthstone you had 400 pounds of gold and did not ask any one to go and help you get it. You came back to Arizona with the California colony and in my own company stood on guard at Fort Cummings, but still you kept "mum." Only last year you say you tried to get there and bring out the kettle of gold. You started with a party from New Mexico but that some Indians drove you

back. Come now let us all take a drink. Now my friend Edwards are you sure that you did not hear as we all did the tale of the two lost men in '58 fixing the boundary line, and imagination runs a long way. Take a good big drink now, it wont hurt you, and do go to Santa Fe and tell that tale there. They will help you. They have not much to do. Just tell it to Staub but it will not go in Tucson. Why it is too fishy even for Charley Brown.

After that scathing indictment, Edwards/Adams left the area never to be heard from again—at least not in this iteration. However, the telling of the tale resurrected interest in the claims of the 1858 gold find by the "real Adams" and the companion named Blair. A man identified as General J.B. Allen then set out to find Blair, who he heard was living in San Bernardino, California, and working at the Paines Hotel. Allen found Blair there, and Blair told him the truth that the whole story was one big joke. Blair's testimony was as follows:

You see we passed going north through the Patagonia mountains and some Mexicans were running one of their adobe smelters with a bellows. I think they call it a baso. Some of the rock must have had copper in it for the slag was full of it and Adams and I broke off some chunks just to fool the other tenderfeet, and when that mescal bad flavored us (and do you know I have never drank that stuff since) and we got left on the Gila just above Steeple Rock we polished them up good in the sand, and when the soldiers found us and took us to the fort we just showed it for a joke, but we never staked a soul with it.

The paper continued that Blair "had two or three pieces left" that he showed to the general. The paragraph concluded, "And it had all come to this! What a vulgar disillusion there was then! No new El Dorado; No happy valley on the Gila with "A POT OF GOLD IN A RING OF ROSES."

The story continued that in 1872, an unnamed prospector showed up in Eastern Arizona claiming he could lead men to a placer mine guarded by the Apache. However, when he failed to lead the men to the mine, they nearly hanged him. Luckily for the man, among the party of prospectors was none other than Anson Pacely Killen Safford, who was the acting governor of Arizona at the time. Safford talked the men out of it, then asked the man what had incited him to make such a foolish decision. He explained,

> As I came in to the territory I stopped in San Bernadino at a hotel kept by a man named "Starkey" which he had bought some time before. An old man who had worked there had died. This man had in the 1850s found a big placer mine in Arizona but it was guarded by Apaches. He showed me nuggets one over two ounces. I had heard and thought much of the tale before this and being in the Bradshaw [mountains] and broke I felt sure, if a big party could be raised and get in the center of the Apache country some of us would find it.

J.H.V. concluded the whole affair thusly,

> And now the story as far as I know it that runs with the Adams Diggings is done, and it does not by any means prove the other tale false. Stranger than fiction so is truth, and without doubt the same search will still go on and may be, someone more lucky than the rest may piece the long looked for spot and find, as was found by he who followed and reached the Arc of the Rainbow, "a pot of gold in a ring of roses."

While this lengthy letter alleged that the whole Adams affair was simply one big joke, by the same token, it's also possible that the letter itself was intended as satire. Or, if not satire, some old timer simply wished to push his own unique theory on the diggings.

13.

ADAMS THE KILLER
STOLEN CALIFORNIA GOLD

Earlier in this book was related E.V. Batchler's version of the Adams legend as he had reconstructed it. In the same FWP report, Batchler then went on to give an account that he admitted was "almost completely at variance" with his story and all other traditional Adams accounts. It came courtesy of Bob Lewis, a Socorro area lawman and sometimes prospector. Lewis painted a very unflattering portrait of Adams, who, according to him, was not only a thief and a liar, but possibly a murderer as well.

According to Lewis's recollection, in August of 1864, Adams and his men were not out gold prospecting, but were out on a fur trapping expedition to catch beaver in northwestern New Mexico.[1] They were headed up to the mountains early to get their camp set up before the cold could set in. It's important to note that what happened next was just Lewis's theory, but Lewis had heard that at that time, a caravan from California carrying between $60-$80,000 in placer gold passed through Fort Wingate on their way to the eastern states. "I know that they [the California caravan] were never seen after the time Adams' party was wiped out by the Indians, so I believe that they camped with Adams' party and met the same fate," Lewis said.[2]

Lewis then went on to accuse Adams of bushwhacking the California caravan and taking their gold. "I know from Adams personal character that he was not above ambushing such a caravan," Lewis said and then went on to add that he believed Adams and his partner, Davidson, had "made plans to hijack the California outfit and steal their gold."[3]

Officers' quarters at Fort Wingate c. 1873. By T.H. O'Sullivan.

Lewis went on to allege that Adams and Davidson got up about two hours before daylight so that "they could go down country a few miles and find a suitable place for waylaying the California outfit." While Lewis could have had Adams and Davidson massacre the California Caravan as planned, instead, Lewis claimed that the Apache had come along and massacred the Californians before Adams ever got there. Adams and Davidson then rejoiced at their great luck in finding the gold unguarded.[4] What followed was not dissimilar to the canyon story, and had Adams and Davidson hide as much of the gold as they could in a safe spot before traveling to Fort Wingate, where they reported the Apache massacre to the authorities. The duo also claimed to have found a rich gold mine in the area that was guarded by the Apache as a cover story for the gold that they would later unearth.

While Lewis's story may be of uncertain veracity, he did at least meet the real Adams—or, if not "The Real McCoy," a man claiming to be Adams—in the 1880s. Lewis said that he came across Adams a second time in the Evans Saloon in Magdalena in March of 1890. There,

> Adams, who had been drinkin' pretty heavy, related a story of how he had gone to Fort [Wingate]… In August, 1864, and petitioned the commanding officer for aid to return to get decent burial to the massacred party and offer him and Davidson protection while they tried to relocate a rich gold claim.[5]

Magdalena, where Lewis lived, seen from a distance, c.1913.

Adams concluded his rant by stating the fort never bothered to help them. As it turned out, in the saloon on that day in March of 1890 was one of the very army officers that Adams was slandering. The man was identified as Captain Sanborn, who stood up and called Adams a liar. Sanborn said that no such incident of Adams coming to the fort, asking for help, and then being denied, ever happened. The drunken Adams then proceeded to threaten Sanborn:

> "Who's a damn liar?" bellowed Adams. "Yuh better eat them words, Cap, or me an' you are agoin' to tangle right here an' now. Bigod! I don't like army officers anyway, so I might as well wipe up th' floor with one of 'em right now."[6]

Bob Lewis, pioneer Magdalena and Socorro officer, came to New Mexico in 1885. He remembers the colorful, dramatic early days well. Above, Mr. Lewis posed with his gun in his shoulder holster, ready for a quick draw. (Redman Photo.)

Bob Lewis as photographed by the *Albuquerque Tribune* on May 23, 1949.

When Adams lunged at Sanborn, the captain countered by grabbing a big butcher knife from behind the counter. At this point Adams ran out the front door with Sanborn chasing him for a couple of blocks, screaming all the while that Adams was the "dirtiest liar that ever lived." Adams fled, and Sanborn returned to the saloon to reiterate that Adams had never been to Fort Wingate.

Lewis claimed to have found proof of the slain gold-bearing caravan from California near Magdalena at a spot called North Lake. Lewis said,

A few miles north of North Lake, I found the bodies of five men, all buried in one hole. I could find no clue to any gold from anything in the vicinity, so I came back to town and reported the finding of the bodies. It is my belief that the bodies I found were the remains of part of Adams expedition, but of course I can't prove this.

Lewis then went on to add that he did know a man named José Maria Jaramillo who had found $20,000 worth of gold buried in that area.[7]

For what it's worth, this story wasn't a one-off, so to speak, and Lewis also told it to Howard Bryan in 1949.[8] However, Lewis was full of questionable stories, as he was among those to claim that Billy the Kid was still alive in the 1940s. Among Lewis's other unique theories was that Black Jack Ketchum had killed Albert J. Fountain in 1896. So, how much credence to give Lewis's account of Adams is debatable.

Chapter Notes

[1] The idea of Adams trapping beaver likely came from the book *Notes of a military reconnaissance, from Fort Leavenworth, in Missouri, to San Diego, in California, including parts of the Arkansas, Del Norte, and Gila rivers* by Lt. W.H. Emory, which related a story about a group of fur trappers in the area coming across gold in the river, and being massacred by Indians. See the chapter "Antecedent to Adams" for more.

[2] Batchler, "Lost Adams," *Lost Treasures and Old Mines*, p.35.

[3] Ibid.

[4] Remember, the Apache cared little for gold and, as such, would not have absconded with it.

[5] Batchler, "Lost Adams," *Lost Treasures and Old Mines*, p.35.

[6] Ibid.

[7] Ibid, p.38.

[8] In *Under the Piñon Tree*, New Mexico writer and former Pie Town resident Jerry D. Thompson stated that it was common knowledge that Adams had stolen his gold from the California Column's wagon train while in Arizona. Thompson, who came of age in Pie Town in the 1950s, recalled stories of Adams being "roughed up" in Reserve and also having been confronted and nearly killed by a former member of the California Column in Magdalena.

Photograph of one of Alvin D. Hudson's expeditions into the malpais to find the diggings, published in the *El Paso Herald* of July 16, 1927.

14.

OUTLAW CANYON

JESSE JAMES AND THE LOST ADAMS

One of the stranger rumors to pervade the Adams myth in the early 1900s was that the canyon was no longer guarded exclusively by the Apache, but by vicious outlaws as well. Among them may have been Jesse James back in the early 1880s—or if not James, some of his gang at least. Most of these outlandish claims involving outlaws were attributed to El Paso old-timers William Donothan and Alvin D. Hudson, who spoke often to the *El Paso Herald* on the diggings in the mid-1920s.

On July 16, 1927, the *Herald* ran a story on Hudson entitled "El Pasoan Plans Search for Lost Adams Diggin's." The article asserted that "renegade white outlaws; murderous San Carlos Apaches, descendants of Geronimo's band; [and] rugged rock," all guarded the Lost Adams canyon. It continued, "These three, outlaws, Apaches and rock, make up the unholy alliance bound together in the common cause of keeping forever secret the exact location in the Malpais mountains of New Mexico of the Lost Adams Diggins, fabled placer mines of untold richness."

J. Frank Dobie must have read this, for he alluded to the possibility of outlaws guarding the canyon in *Apache Gold & Yaqui Silver*, writing that certain people "told of a nest of desperate outlaws allied with a few never yet subjugated

Jesse James

Apaches and Navajos who from a secret oasis in the malpais guard the only entrance and kill any stranger who tries to enter."[1]

Likewise, a fear of renegade outlaws and Indians was part of the impetus for a 1927 Adams hunt taking place from the air rather than the ground. The expedition backer, a man known only as Baker, explained to their hired pilot that not only would an aerial expedition be swifter, but safer. Baker argued, "It is hazardous flying country, but far more dangerous for the ground traveler. The section where we want to go is inhabited by bandits, outlaws and renegade Indians."[2]

Baker got his information straight from Hudson, who was also involved, albeit only tangentially, to the aerial expedition of 1927, which folded with a plane crash and a loss of finances. But where did Hudson get his information? As it was, Hudson had a tie to the diggings in the form of two uncles that he believed found the canyon in the early 1880s. The uncles, Frank and Willa Lee of Iowa, were taken to the canyon by a 19-year-old African-American man in 1881. The men were attacked by the sentries of the canyon, with Willa being killed. Frank was only wounded, and with the aid of the guide, he was able to escape with only a punctured lung.

According to the article, back home in Iowa, Frank told his family of the ordeal. Rather than Indians, he implied it was the James Gang that attacked them:

> There to the members of the family circle he recounted the adventures he and his brother had had in the territory of New Mexico. He told of a box canyon into which there was only one opening, a narrow pass, and of the

renegades, including members of Jesse James's own gang, who inhabited the place.[3]

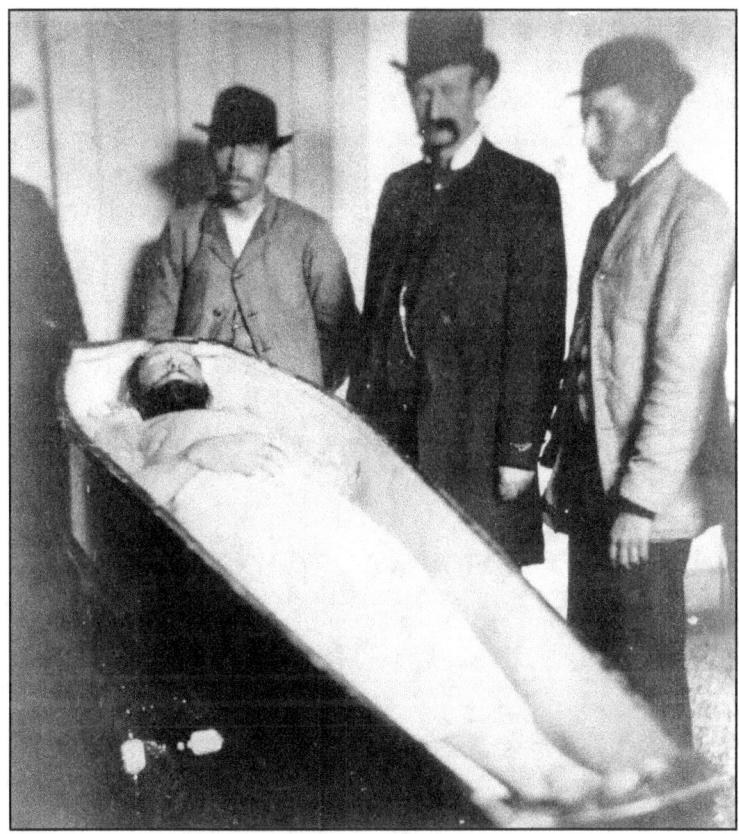

Jesse James post-mortem in 1882.

Unfortunately it was never elaborated upon who of Jesse James's gang was in the canyon or why. Then of course there's the small matter that Jesse James himself was dead by the spring of 1882. However, for what it's worth, Jesse James did occasionally visit New Mexico, and on one occasion met with Billy the Kid in Las Vegas. According to Henry Hoyt in his memoir *Frontier Doctor*, he observed the Kid, who he knew, with James at a casino there. James was rumored to be visiting the territory for a new hideout or base of operations. This was in the year 1879, but could James or some of his gang have discovered Sno-Ta-hay Canyon at some point?

While that's a long shot, at least one tale placed James nearer the country of the diggings than Las Vegas, which is in northeastern New Mexico. Specifically, James was reported once in Hillsboro, which was located near other gold boomtowns like Kingston. An old timer there known only as Old Spike had claimed to have ridden with Quantrill's Raiders during the Civil War. As such, Od Spike knew Jesse James and was shocked to encounter him one day in the New Mexico desert in either 1880 or 1881, prior to James's 1882 assassination.

Hillsboro depicted on an old postcard.

Old Spike was digging for gold north of a town called Gold Dust when he spied a rider in the distance. It turned out to be his old acquaintance, Jesse James, who informed him he was hiding from the law. Old Spike showed James to a secluded cave he knew of in the region, which James was said to hide in for a few weeks. When things cooled down, he stayed for a time in Old Spike's home and even accompanied him into Hillsboro a few times. James told Old Spike he was giving up his outlaw ways and heading for California. Of course, as we all know, James was shot by Robert Ford in April of 1882, but as far as Old Spike was concerned, the last he saw of James, he was headed west of Hillsboro.[4]

While west of Hillsboro was indeed the land of the Lost Adams, James stumbling across the canyon seems unlikely. If there are any kernels of truth of the James Gang haunting the canyon, it may simply boil down to James taking a few trips to New Mexico. Beyond that, maybe some outlaws briefly took possession of the gold-encrusted canyon visited by the Lee brothers, who perhaps merely assumed the outlaw band was that of the James Gang.

More tales of outlaws in the canyon came about from an 1896 excursion into the malpais by Edward Kneezell, an El Paso architect who had befriended a half-breed Apache who agreed to take him to the rim of Sno-Ta-Hay Canyon. Assuming the man was telling the truth, from the north rim of the canyon looking down into it he observed a stream and the ruins of the cabin. More interesting, though, was his statement that he spied a more

Alvin D. Hudson hunting the diggings (*El Paso Herald,* July 16, 1927).

modern encampment. His guide told him that it belonged to "white men wanted by the law of the outside world" who "lived in safety, jealously guarding the gold that was there and the narrow pass into the canyon with rifles and sixguns."[5] The guide also stated that "a few roving San Carlos Apaches, survivors of Geronimo's followers, camped in the valley."[6]

Hudson, who also recounted the above story, concluded his tale of the outlaw-infested canyon to the *Herald* with the following statement:

For 70 years or more those mountains have been the rendezvous of desperate men and savage Apaches. Jesse James and his men once hid there and I have some accurate information which leads me to believe that James was never killed as he was supposed to have been. The malpies are still inhabited by moonshiners and Apaches and anyone who goes into them must be ready for anything. Someday I am going in, however, if I have to ask the government for a troop of soldiers to clean out the place once and for all.

Perhaps lending just a little credence to the idea that outlaws at one time occupied the canyon was an account from William Donothan. He claimed in the past to have found the entrance to the canyon, which he stated had four lines of barbed wire strung across it. Barbed wire was something more common to the white man than the Apache, so perhaps it was strung up by a group of outlaws?

Chapter Notes

[1] Dobie, *Apache Gold & Yaqui Silver*, p.117.
[2] Phillips, "A Pilot's Opinion of the Lost Adams," *Gold!* (Fall 1975), p.25.
[3] "El Pasoan Plans Search for Lost Adams Diggin's," *El Paso Herald* (July 16, 1927).
[4] Raynor, *Old Timers Talk in Southwestern New Mexico*, pp.36-38.
[5] "El Pasoan Plans Search for Lost Adams Diggin's," *El Paso Herald* (July 16, 1927).
[6] Ibid.

15.

ANTECEDENTS TO ADAMS
PRE-ADAMS DISCOVERERS

As it stands, 1864 is the most widely accepted date for Adams and his men discovering the diggings. However, some sources placed Adams finding the diggings prior to that, even as early as the 1850s. Other stories also told of strikingly similar accounts that not only predated Adams, but which didn't include him at all. The most notable of these was recounted in *Lost Mines of the Great Southwest* by John D. Mitchell. In the book, Mitchell put forth the theory that the Lost Adams were in the vicinity of the headwaters of the Prieto (Black) River north of Silver City. As evidence, he used the writings of Lieutenant W.H. Emory, who had his journals published in 1848 as *Notes of a Military Reconnaissance from Fort Leavenworth in Kansas to San Diego, California.*

> The Prieto (Black) River flows down from the mountains freighted with gold. Its sands are said to be full of this precious metal. A few adventurers who ascended the river hunting beaver washed the sands at night when they halted and were richly rewarded for their trouble. Tempted by their success, they made a second trip and were attacked and most of them killed by the Indians. My authority for the statement is Landeau, who, though an illiterate man, is truthful.[1]

The above quotation came from a journal entry created on October 26, 1846, long before Adams ever set foot in New Mexico. Unfortunately, Emory never mentioned the gold streak again, nor the names of the men associated with it apart from Landeau, who was not mentioned again in his diary. Nor was anyone named Adams mentioned, by the way, despite what a few others have written.

Interestingly, later iterations of the Adams story sometimes integrated aspects of Emory's notes by making Adams a fur trapper. Bob Lewis, for instance, mentioned Adams trapping beaver, as did the pulp article "Apache Gold" by George Dillon. Something quasi-similar to the Emory account popped up courtesy of a letter written by George R. Spooner published in the *Arizona Republican* on March 11, 1898. It set the Adams story in 1850 and also mentioned the Black River as a notable landmark.

Jack Purcell dug up another Adams antecedent, which read like a more down-to-earth, less adventurous version of the Lost Adams. It took place in 1862, two years before the traditional Adams account. Not only did it take place earlier, but it comprised a completely different cast of characters.

It was written by Daniel Ellis Connor, a contemporary of Adams, in his book *Joseph Reddeford Walker and the Arizona Adventure*. Connor's account told of being one of about thirty to forty soldiers under the command of Joseph Reddeford Walker, who came into New Mexico from Colorado in about 1862. They stopped in Santa Fe to get permission from the military commander for the Department of New Mexico and Arizona, which at that time was General Carlton. Specifically, they asked Carlton's permission to go to Arizona to mine for gold. Permission was granted, and later, while at Pinos Altos, Connor heard tales of a Mexican man who had been a captive of the Apache. The unnamed man had been telling stories of a murder involving a California man who had found a large quantity of gold in a canyon with a peculiar Z shape. However, if you're thinking that this man was Connor's equivalent of Gotch Ear, that wasn't exactly the case, as Connor never met the man—he only heard his adventurous tale.

There are whispers that Sno-Ta-Hay Canyon might have been mined by the Spaniards hundreds of years before Adams was even born. Some pointed to a mysterious stone symbol near Reserve, New Mexico, a frequent stop for Adams hunters, as evidence. Richard French was the first to relate the stone to Adams in his book *Four Days from Fort Wingate*.

Sometime in the late 1970s, Bob Gordon heard of a treasure map "carved on the surface of a large flat rock." Said map supposedly led to an old Spanish mine in the vicinity of Black Bull Peak which was southwest of Reserve. Being practically on the state line with Arizona, it was as likely a spot to find the Adams diggings as anywhere. The stone map was said to be located near a lookout tower on an isolated mountain summit and was thought to have been carved by the Spanish during their occupation. Richard French spoke of Gordon showing him a picture of the map in 1981:

> [Gordon] showed us photographs they had taken of the unusual boulder with the drawing etched across its surface. The idea of such a map carved on a block of stone and sitting on top of a high peak in that isolated region held a certain amount of mystery of its own.
> [French, *Four Days From Fort Wingate*, p.133]

After this, French asked around Reserve, which it should be noted is the county seat of the sparsely populated Catron County, about the map. He said that most of the residents had at least heard of it, but none were sure who had carved it or when other than it had always been there. Could it be another clue to the Lost Adams? *Quién Sabe?*

However, Connor and his comrades eventually did meet a twenty-year-old half-breed Apache chieftain that they called Charlie, who agreed to lead the men to a canyon in Arizona with a huge quartz vein of gold. Like Gotch Ear, Charlie was right and the canyon did indeed contain gold even if perhaps his claims were somewhat exaggerated. Connor called the canyon Haviamp, and this is what he had to say about the gold there:

We spent the following day in a more thorough examination of the bed of the Haviamp to determine the character and extent of its gold production, and was pleased with the prospect. One day after another added confidence and resulted in the final decision that there was gold in this creek in paying quantities and there was plenty deer and other game in the woods. This being settled, the next thing to be done was the building of a permanent corral with which to secure the mules at night and to do away with the necessity of standing around them all night continuously, as we had been doing constantly for the last nine months. We had but one axe and by first one and another, it was kept in constant use felling large pine trees one after another in the same direction, upon each other, and we had a long rectangular corral, constructed with whole trees, which were too large to be moved or broken through. This was the stoutest corral ever built in central Arizona and when the stock was once into it, they might be killed, but there was no such thing as storming them out of it. The next move made was the holding of a miners' meeting. Being only twenty-six of us, there was not much discussion. The district was first defined by bounding it by the distant ridges and primary ranges of the country, without any trouble of any measurement. A mining claim was defined and declared to be one hundred yards of an ore vein or quartz-lode, and the same extent on a creek bed in surface or placer diggings. The claimant was to hold all the ground on either side of the creek in placer diggings and on either side of the vein if it was a quartz ledge for a distance of fifty yards, thereby constituting a claim of one hundred yards square, lying upon the "pay streak" whether of quartz or surface mines. The claimant was to own the possessory right and title to "all of the earth and minerals therein contained." It was further provided that each member of our party should be entitled to two claims each, upon all discoveries of any character of mines whatever—one by the right of discovery and the other by virtue of pre-emption.[2]

A bit later in the journal, Connor described building the famous cabin common to all Adams accounts:

My three messmates and myself concluded to build a stout log house which would be convenient for a fort in case of necessity for self-defense. We finished one in about two weeks, built of logs three feet in diameter and covered with stout timbers upon which we put pine boughs and lastly a foot of dirt which rendered it fireproof, but if it ever became waterproof it was after I left the country. This was the first house built by any of our party and consequently the first ever built in central Arizona that we know of, by the Anglo-Saxon. We now devoted our time to hunting and prospecting when not at work upon our claims. Trees were felled, out of which the ordinary rocker was constructed for washing gold. Rude planks which were split out with an axe had to serve our purpose and such implements as could be made out of such materials for mining purposes were pretty soon in operation. The diggings did not yield near our expectations, but it was enough to convince us that we were in a gold region where the best of mines might be found. The Apaches began to visit us. They seemed not to know anything of our efforts to make a treaty with [the] Irotaba [tribe]. They importuned us by long and senseless speeches to go with them upon a "big" bear hunt. They were troublesome only for a short time, for they went to war with us and that ended their visits. One of our party imprudently kicked one of them out of his way while cooking his supper after a tiresome day's tramp and the whole batch of them immediately left the camp in great indignation and never returned again."[3]

Unrelated illustration of soldiers attacking Apache herders in a canyon setting.

And with that, Connor's account of the less than spectacular gold canyon came to an end. No Apache massacre, no odyssey across the desert—nothing. This historical account was written by Connor for his memoirs when he later moved to Cincinnati, Ohio, where he served as the city engineer. After that, in the 1870s, he became a city engineer in the Los Angeles area, where Adams would also have lived at the time. Jack Purcell put forth the intriguing theory that Adams may have heard Connor's tale firsthand and lifted it to become what may have simply been a fictional version of the Lost Adams Diggings. More specifically, the idea was that while Adams may have found a gold placer somewhere in New Mexico, the actual events encompassing its discovery may have been entirely made up. This would have been done to disguise the exact location of the diggings, or so the theory went. Whether related or not, Connor's story is suspiciously similar to that of the Lost Adams.

Chapter Notes

---

[1] Emory, *Notes of a Military Reconnaissance*, p.66.
[2] Connor, *Joseph Reddeford Walker*, pp 99-100.
[3] Ibid, p.105.

Governor Miguel Antonio Otero c.1902.

16.

THE GOVERNOR & THE GOLD
MIGUEL OTERO HUNTS THE ADAMS

In addition to Billy the Kid, the Kid's "pal" Governor Miguel A. Otero also hunted the Lost Adams Diggings. Unlike many "pals" of William H. Bonney, Otero had far more claims to fame than just knowing the Kid. Otero was part of a rich railroad family that frequently traveled the West before settling in the wild town of Las Vegas, New Mexico. This is where Otero befriended a jailed Billy the Kid in 1880. Like the Kid, Otero was a staunch opponent of the dreaded Santa Fe Ring, a group of corrupt politicians that secretly ruled New Mexico Territory. Otero fought with them both inside and outside of the political realm.

Politically, he was an adversary of the Santa Fe Ring during his terms as Governor of New Mexico Territory from 1897 to 1906. Outside of the political arena, the Santa Fe Ring once illegally seized the Otero family mine, called Nuestra Senora de los Delores, located in Santa Fe County. With 162 miners in their employ, the Ring had taken possession of the mine and turned it into a fort of sorts. Otero and a dozen or so allies snuck into the mine by lowering themselves by rope down an old abandoned 85-foot mine shaft. Taking the miners by surprise, these dozen or so men evicted the trespassers who greatly outnumbered them from the mine. After expelling the Ring physically, Otero next battled them in the courtroom and won, reclaiming his family mine legally.

In addition to the mine he owned, Otero also hunted up a few lost ledges of gold. One was hidden somewhere in the Sangre de Cristo Mountains and had been brought to Otero's attention by a friend who brought him a sample of ore. Though he agreed to take Otero to this lost ledge of ore, he died before he could do so as knowledgeable prospectors are wont to do in treasure tales. If an article from the early 1900s is to be believed, Otero also tried his hand at finding the Lost Adams Diggings.

Political cartoon depicting the Santa Fe Ring.

The *San Juan County Index* reported on this interesting rumor on May 27, 1904:

After Famous Adams Diggings.
A pretty story is being told in Albuquerque today to the effect that Gov. M. A. Otero and Secretary of Territory J. W. Reynolds have gone south to hunt for the famous lost Adams diggings, which, some prospectors say, are located in the Cuchillo Negras of Sierra county. The governor and secretary went south the other evening, and a little mischievous bird tells The Citizen that they

are out hunting for hidden treasures, which, according to advice which they had previously received, they expected to find. These Adams diggings have cost many a poor prospector his life, and during the bloody days of twenty odd years ago, when Victorio and Geronimo rode rough shod over the southern counties with their bands of renegade Apaches, only a few of the most daring white prospectors ventured out in search of these supposed fabulously rich placers, and they never returned to civilization to give an account of their trip.

Circumstances have changed since then—Victorio, Geronimo and the blood thirsty bands have been whipped into submission, some being killed, and these diggings may yet be found. Who knows but that Governor Otero and Secretary Reynolds may find them? If there is a smile on their faces when they return north in a few days, it will be an indication that they have located the wonderful gold producing placers; but if not—don't say anything to them about the Adams diggings.—Albuquerque Citizen.

Unfortunately, Otero didn't mention his alleged Adams hunt in his memoirs, *My Nine Years as Governor of the Territory of New Mexico, 1897-1906*. Was it merely a rumor? And, if not, had Governor Otero found the massive gold vein would he have shared some of it with the territory he governed, or would he have added Adams' gold to the family fortune? In any case, he was certainly one of the better-known figures to hunt the diggings.

THE "LOST ADAMS" DIGGINGS.

A Party of California Adventurers Hunting After Placer Mines.

SANTA FE, N. M., Dec. 3.—Old man Adams of the "Lost Adams" gold diggings with a party of adventurers from California, who have a physician with them, to look after Adams' health arrived at Navajo Springs a few days ago and after a day's rest started on a hunt for the diggings. Adams is under the impression that the lost mines are about one hundred and twenty miles south of Gallup and the Californians are accompanying him with the view of ascertaining the truthfulness of the story. He claims to have discovered twenty years ago near the Arizona and New Mexican line, placer beds of fabulous va'ue, but was prevented from working them because of the hostile Apaches.

The *Butte City Daily Miner* of December 4, 1889.

17.

ADAMS RIDES AGAIN
AN IMPOSTOR OR THE REAL MCCOY?

Although it was commonly accepted that Adams passed away in September of 1886 per the account of Captain Shaw, contemporary newspaper reports of the time disagreed. Not that newspapers back then were pillars of accountability, but their words should still not be ignored. As early as August 22, 1886, a small blurb ran in the general news roundup of the *Albuquerque Journal* stating that "A.V. Adams, the discoverer of the lost Adams diggings, is not dead, but is alive and hearty." Following that report was the *Silver City Enterprise,* which wrote in their December 7, 1888 issue:

> The papers of the territory are in error in stating that Adams of "Adams Diggins" fame is dead. He is now living in Encinada [sic], near San Diego. He has already spent three fortunes seeking for the lost diggings and hopes to be able to find them yet or spend another fortune in the attempt.

Among those who had contact with Adams the year he was alleged to have died was Colonel Jack Fleming of Silver City. In 1886, he traveled to San Diego in an attempt to hire a team to take him into old Mexico on a gold hunt. There, he encountered Adams running a stable in San Diego.[1] The two spoke mutual acquaintances they had in Silver City and eventually Fleming caught on that this was THE Adams.

Notably, Fleming's iteration of Adams was a bit more humble than his counterparts. "Adams assured me," Fleming said, "that the tale of him taking out a large amount of gold was all a mere tale of someone's imagination but that had he been able to return to the diggings the tale might have become a fact."[2]

Fleming pitched Adams the idea of forming a company of 100 men, each of whom would put up $200 to finance a new expedition for the diggings. Adams, perhaps having been on too many failed ventures already, was reluctant "because he feared the others would become discouraged if [they] did not find the gold immediately." However, Adams relented to the expedition so long as Fleming actually incited enough interest and capital in it.

Apparently Fleming's visit got Adams' old desires to itching again. Upon returning to Silver City, one of Fleming's friends, identified as John Reed, told him that he had already been approached by a "company organized by Adams himself to renew the search."

Fleming said,

> I advised him to go on with the party because I believed Adams to be a straightforward honest and upright man of his word. Reed went with them but I have never heard of them finding anything. The last time I heard of Adams was in Clifton, Arizona, where there are some gold diggings but not the original Adams diggings.

There is at least a paper trail alluding to this statement, though not until 1889 when papers began recording that Adams was heading east from California yet again to rediscover the diggings. (Or, if not Adams, perhaps an impostor?) *The East Las Vegas Daily Optic* reported on October 11, 1889, the first rumblings of a new expedition to the diggings:

> The lost Adams placers in Arizona still continue to inspire occasional adventurous fools with the hope of discovering them. A party had been organized at

Pasadena, California, to go on this fool's errand. The mines are supposed to be somewhere near the line of the Atlantic & Pacific road."[3]

Typical desert rat prospector on the trail.

As it turned out, and though he wasn't mentioned, in the party was the thought dead Adams. Later, the *Western Liberal* of November 1, 1889, reported on what they called "The Mysterious Seven," a group of prospectors led by Adams himself:

> The original "Adams," who lost a bonanza years ago, came into town Tuesday with a party and from what can be learned the lost Adams diggings will soon materialize in this vicinity. Nothing can be learned except that they are the parties who are determined as the "mysterious seven" by the Tucson Citizen recently, and of whom nothing could be learned when they were equipping themselves at Tucson by the reporters of the dailies of that city.[4]

Adams and the party next popped up in the newspapers in December. Stories were published in numerous papers, but this particular blurb was taken from the *Butte City Daily Miner* of December 4, 1889:

Santa Fe, N. M. Dec. 3.—Old man Adams of the "Lost Adams" gold diggings with a party of adventurers from California, who have a physician with them, to look after Adams' health arrived at Navajo Springs a few days ago and after a day's rest started on a hunt for the diggings. Adams is under the impression that the lost mines are about one hundred and twenty miles south of Gallup and the Californians are accompanying him with the view of ascertaining the truthfulness of the story.

What this Adams-led excursion resulted in is unknown, but it obviously didn't lead to the lost diggings. In the spring of 1890, a highly sensationalized lost Adams search did occur on a Navajo reservation, but Adams himself was not a part of it. Besides that, was the man who returned to Arizona in 1889 really Adams? It's possible that Colonel Fleming either misremembered the date of his meeting with Adams or that perhaps he spoke with Adams early in 1886. This would have allowed Adams time to travel to New Mexico and suffer a heart attack as Captain Shaw often stated. As to the "Adams" reported in 1889, not much was said of him, so perhaps he was simply an impostor?[5]

In a July 2, 1927, *El Paso Herald* piece, an old Indian fighter named John L. Riggs claimed Adams lived to be 95. This could imply that Adams lived to see the 20th Century. The same article also quoted a Silver City stagecoach driver named William Bates, still living in 1927. The article stated, "If Adams is dead, Bates has never heard of his death."

Did Adams live past his September 1886 expiration date? Unless someone was pretending to be Adams, which did happen from time to time, it would seem that Adams lived on, and his real death date is unknown.

Chapter Notes

---

[1] This gelled with other reports that Adams ran a stable, albeit in Los Angeles.

[2] I retrieved this story from an undated newspaper clipping in a folder on "Lost Treasures" housed in the Historical Society for Southeast New Mexico Archives in Roswell, NM. As such, I know not the exact paper it came from, nor the publication date.

[3] *East Las Vegas Daily Optic* (October 11, 1889).

[4] *Western Liberal* (November 1, 1889).

[5] There is one other possibility, which is that perhaps the 1889 excursion actually killed Adams—or, if not Adams, the old man pretending to be him. As it was back then, "old-timers" weren't terribly good at remembering dates. If you'll recall, an old-timer only identified as Johnson claimed to meet with Adams on his deathbed after Adams came down sick in a snowstorm on a return trip to the diggings. An intense snowstorm hit the region in the winter of early 1890, so perhaps this was the incident Johnson spoke of?

MUST FIND ANOTHER REASON FOR THE EARTHQUAKES

Socorro Mining Expert Says There Have Been No Slips in Strata of the Magdalena Mountains.

The *Albuquerque Morning Journal* of August 23, 1906.

18.

THE DIGGINGS DESTROYED
WHY THE CANYON CANNOT BE FOUND

For many years, the Spaniards labored under the belief that New Mexico harbored the mythical Seven Cities of Gold. Even after the numerous misidentifications of various pueblos and false leads, it took a long, long time for belief in the Seven Cities to die out. And if there was any shred of a doubt that some small remnant of the cities ever existed, they were washed away in the advent of satellite mapping, which finally revealed all the desert had for years concealed. In some ways, the same should be true of the Adams Diggings. Or, that is to say that modern mapping technology should have been able to conclusively determine the spot of the diggings. Unless, that is, the canyon was destroyed in a cataclysm.

This belief is a fairly popular one, and was even used as the climax of *Mackenna's Gold* when the canyon collapsed upon itself. Coincidentally, James McKenna, no relation to the movie, propagated the theory that the diggings had been destroyed in his book *Black Range Tales*. McKenna's source was Jason Baxter, who was of the opinion that the Snively Diggings, the Schaeffer Diggins, and the Adams Diggings were all the same. Unlike Adams, Baxter had a mind for mapping and could easily find landmarks in the most barren landscapes. Having heard the story of all three diggings, Baxter set out to find them himself in the mid-1870s. He found Adams' same canyon, charred cabin remains and all until he, too, was chased out by a roving band of Apache.

HIDDEN BY THE APACHE

Rather than a natural disaster, others thought that the Apache themselves concealed the canyon. In "Prospector Spends 40 Years Hunting Lost Adams Diggin's," published in the *El Paso Herald* on August 13, 1927, a man identified only as Johnson suggested that the diggings were "covered up by Indians, all trace of them obliterated with rock and dirt, for fear that white men would carry away the gold which has been the heritage of each successive generation of tribesmen since time immemorial." Notably, Johnson claimed to have spoken to Adams on his deathbed in the 1870s. Johnson believed that "the Indian chiefs gave orders to take out no more of the gold and to cover up the Diggins." Johnson said he asked an old Indian acquaintance why they didn't mine more gold from the canyon once, and the Indian responded, "If we did, white men would get it."

In 1884, Baxter told his tale to McKenna and mounted another campaign to find the diggings, which they set out to do the next year. Though Baxter managed to find his way back to the precise location, the landscape had been altered in the last decade. For instance, Baxter thought the landmark known as Island Mountain had been destroyed. McKenna related:

> Baxter rode ahead to look for the opening into the park. When we came up we found him staring around him like one in a daze. And no wonder! The whole mountain looked as if it had been crushed by giant hands, as a child would crush a snowball. Even the ridge was broken in many places. Not a sign of a tree or an animal could be seen in any direction. Immense boulders lay tumbled together as if they had crashed in a mighty battle, scattering splinters in every direction. Following the broken ridge we came to the spot where Baxter expected to find the opening to the park. Instead of the park we came into a barren gulch filled in places almost to the top with rocks and debris. No water. No vegetation. No animals. No mineral.
>
> "This sure beats hell!" was all Baxter could find to say. We went along the sides of the gulch looking for a level stretch to camp, but there was none. "This mountain

looks as if it had busted open in a big explosion," said Poland, and it was all that was said by any of us as we climbed over the rocks and the debris.[1]

A.M. Tenney Junior's account of the Adams story published in the *El Paso Herald* in 1928 implied that the landscape had changed due to fire. In this case it was Captain Shaw rather than Adams who stated this opinion. Shaw was trying to locate a distinctive tree "that had grown out of the ground to a height of about three feet and then had been bent over and groaned horizontally for about twelve feet before turning up again." Shaw believed that this tree held the key to re-finding the canyon. "But timber fires had swept over much of the mountains since Shaw said he had been there before and nothing seemed to look familiar to him..."

A bit later, when looking for another landmark that Baxter identified as Pink Hill, Baxter theorized, "From what I see the Lost Diggin's are now in a Lost Canyon, scattered more likely to the head of the Little Colorado River."[2] Baxter continued,

> "It seems to me that first there came a quake which pretty near shook the mountain to pieces, and then cloudburst that carried away whatever gold or mineral was in the canyon. Even the rocks look strange, mostly a burnt out lava and a species of diorite. The Pink Hill may have been a volcanic vent, producing gold. The mineral zone must have been small or we'd be able to

find extensions nearby, but you can see for yourselves there's nothing here but lava, or malpais. In time someone may locate a valuable copper mine in the canyon with the blue-stained shale, but it's not for us."[3]

Out of the West

Did an Earthquake Cover the Adams 'Diggings'?

by BILL McGAW

The *El Paso Herald Post* of February 17, 1962.

"Boys, we sure came to Lost Canyon Diggins," Baxter said. "There'll never be any yellow nuggets found here unless there comes another earthquake and cloudburst to throw and wash back into the gulch what they took out of it."[4] Baxter then suggested that perhaps next spring they could return and see if the landscape had been altered further in a positive way instead of a negative one.

However, though Baxter had been the best-known source for the diggings having been destroyed, he wasn't the only one to propose this idea. And, nor was *Black Range Tales* the first publication to put the idea in print. The *Boston Sunday Post's* article, "A Lost Gold Mine," published on September 19, 1897, put forth a theory as to how the diggings were lost via a blacksmith in Duncan, Arizona, who claimed to have known Adams:

"Now, I've got a theory how those diggings were lost. A year ago I had as nice a little ranch as you ever laid eyes on. Just across the river there, I had a big garden with all kinds of truck growing in it. As handsome a little place as you ever saw in your life. Well, one night there came a cloudburst up in the mountains back there, and down came the gravel and boulders and buried my garden out of sight Why, there are rocks over there weighing tons standing where my garden stood."

Just here there was a man passing by and the old blacksmith hailed him in this fashion out of the gloom:

"I say, Bill, how deep do you think the gravel is over on my garden across the river?"

Out of the darkness came the answer back:

"Oh, about two feet I should reckon."

"Now, that's the way old man Adams lost his diggings. A cloudburst just changed the whole aspect of everything; swept the shack away and turned everything upside down."

Though some researchers have suggested that no severe earthquakes had taken place in western New Mexico for many centuries, this isn't exactly true. While I could find no mention of significant earthquakes in the region between 1875-1885 to line up with Baxter's story, the Socorro region suffered earthquakes in 1906. The *Albuquerque Morning Journal* of August 23, 1906, reported that residents were indeed feeling earth tremors in the early 1900s. Furthermore, photographs even exist attesting to the damage done by the earthquakes of 1906, such as the one above, which shows the damage done to the Socorro Courthouse in a 1906 earthquake.

Charles Allen was also of the opinion that Adams believed the landscape of the canyon had irrevocably been changed due to weather. Allen wrote, "Adams was of the opinion that a waterspout had washed trees, boulders, and rubbish to the box canyon, choking it and filling the canyon above the dam so formed with debris."

Just such a waterspout hit Socorro County on August 19, 1896. The next day, the *Santa Fe New Mexican* reported that twenty men were missing, having been swept away in the torrent, and that only two bodies of the dead so far had been found. Not only that, but thirty homes in the Mogollon region had been swept away.

Likewise, the *Socorro Chieftain* of January 9, 1904, wrote of the diggings that "Any mountainous country is subject to great changes in the lapse of years, and it is probable that all traces of the original workings are covered deep with soil from the wash of the surrounding hills."

Apache Spirit Dancers as photographed by Katherine Taylor Dodge c. 1899. The four dancers represented the four cardinal directions—north, south, east, and west, while the fifth dancer served as the clown who protected the others by driving away evil spirits.

Whether it was via earthquake or deluge, it would seem an Act of God may have indeed hidden the diggings.[5] Actually, this would hold with the Apache spiritual view of things. Though the Apache have what are called Mountain Spirits, they have only one creator God, that being Ussen, who just so happens to be associated with gold. When it came to gold, the Apache had no problem with the white man picking it up if the earth had already yielded it. If the white man dug into the earth to get it, that was another matter. The daughter of the Apache leader Perico, Darlene Enjady, explained to Eve Ball that "You can pick it up off the ground, but you mustn't dig for it because the Mountain Spirits would get mad and make an earthquake."[6]

Actually, the white man's love of gold is tied into some Apache creation stories. Ball wrote of this in *Indeh*, stating how the son of Ussen, Child of Water, came to Earth to give the Apache herbs for medicine and weapons. To the White Eyes, or Anglos, Child of Water gave the pick and the shovel:

> It was what he gave them that caused all the trouble. With the pick and shovel the prospectors grubbed in the body of Mother Earth for forbidden gold and caused the mountains to dance and shake their shoulders. Mother Earth opened up and swallowed whole villages.[7]

No wonder the Apache despised the unearthing of gold. Perhaps had the prospectors dug into the main vein that resided just beyond the falls in Sno-Ta-Hay Canyon, a great earthquake would have befallen all of Apacheria? This was actually alluded to in an article in the *El Paso Herald* published on August 6, 1927. Sandy Welch, an old Scotsman who lived near the canyon, said that the placer "was sacred to the Indian gods and the superstitious tribesmen could not well take the chances of incurring divine wrath by letting the white man remove any large amount of the gold."

Whether the diggings were destroyed, or if by some miracle they still lay hidden in the desert, at this point, the truth will pale in comparison to the legend that they have spawned.

Chapter Notes

---

[1] McKenna, *Black Range Tales*, p.62

[2] Ibid.

[3] Ibid, p.63.

[4] Ibid.

[5] In one of his 1927 articles appearing in the *El Paso Herald*, Alvin D. Hudson gave two separate accounts of men who were taken to what he believed to be Sno-Ta-Hay Canyon. Notably, on both occasions, the visitors were taken by an Indian guide to the rim of the canyon to look down into it. If we were to try and marry these two events, one might surmise that the earthquake destroyed the entrance to the canyon without destroying the diggings entirely. This might explain why the two men were taken to the ridge of the canyon as opposed to being led through the "Secret Door," which perhaps had been destroyed? And, although one of the men was led out of the canyon via a secret exit, it was never described by him as being in a "zigzag" or z-shaped pattern. As such, it could be that the canyon didn't entirely collapse into itself, but simply that the famous "Secret Door" had been covered or destroyed, necessitating a new way into Sno-Ta-Hay Canyon.

[6] Robinson, *Apache Voices*, p.110.

[7] Ball, *Indeh*, p.99.

LOST ADAMS BIBLIOGRAPHY

What follows is an attempt at a comprehensive Lost Adams bibliography. I say attempt because these are all of the books featuring the diggings that I have come across, though inevitably there are obscure titles parked on dusty old library shelves throughout the Southwest that I have no knowledge of. Most of these I have read, aside from a few that proved either too elusive or too expensive to purchase. Nor are little tomes like the W.H. Byerts pamphlet covered again since they were chronicled in the first chapter.

Bryan, Howard. *True Tales of the American Southwest: Pioneer Recollections of Frontier Adventures.* **(Clear Light Publishers, 1998) 286 p.** Though there's plenty of interesting historical portraits painted by Howard Bryan in his book, the one of interest relating to the Lost Adams was conducted with Bob Lewis. Though initially reluctant to talk of Adams and the diggings, Lewis eventually did. The chapter also offers an intriguing perspective of a reporter interested in the diggings trying to interview a reluctant subject. Spanning pages 33-54, the interview is loaded with information.

Childress, David Hatcher. *Lost Cities and Ancient Mysteries of the Southwest* **(Adventures Unlimited Press, 2009) 576 p.** Author/adventurer David Hatcher Childress discusses the diggings from pages 393-404. He gives his own interesting pastiche based on accounts he'd heard. And, while stopped in Reserve, New Mexico, he heard locals talk of an old settlement/post office named "Adams Diggings".

Conrotto, Eugene L. *Lost Gold and Silver Mines of the Southwest* **(Dover, 1963/1991) 250 p.** Though it covers a multitude of treasure caches, they all stem from entries from *Desert* magazine. Some of the entries are detailed and well-done, but the entry on Adams is skimpy to say the least. The two entries are limited to page 32, and one consists of the account of Lieutenant W.H. Emory and erroneously claims that it mentioned Adams when it never did. The second entry is unrelated, and tells of a man named Adams who found gold nuggets in Arizona in 1925.

Drago, Harry Sinclair. *Lost Bonanzas: Tales of the Legendary Lost Mines of the American West* **(Bramhall House, 1966) 276 p.** Contains two chapters on the Lost Adams, Chapter 18: "Lost Adams Diggings" and Chapter 19: "The Searchers," totaling 26 pages. For the most part, the author regurgitates Dobie, but adds in a few details of his own. If he was just filling in blanks and making assumptions or if he discovered a few new nuggets is unknown.

French, Richard. *Four Days From Fort Wingate: The Lost Adams Diggings* **(Caxton Printers, Ltd., 1994) 260 p.** A well organized book that gives the accounts of Dobie and others, with supplementary history on gold in New Mexico in general for added interest. As a love letter to the Lost Adams by one who searched for it, it's a good read either for beginners or completists. It also turns up a few interesting nuggets of its own, such as the strange rock marker outside of Reserve, NM.

--------*Return to the Lost Adams Diggings* **(2014) 322 p.** This book chronicles Paul A. Hayle's search for the Adams Diggings, which he thinks he found in the mountains near the Double H Ranch. Whether the location was really that of Sno-Ta-Hay Canyon or not, his adventures were certainly interesting.

Jameson, W.C. *New Mexico Treasure Tales* **(Caxton Press, 2003) 200 p.** As the title suggests, a collection of treasure caches set in New Mexico. The book is broken up into sections including: Northwest, Northeast, Southeast and Southwest. The entry on the diggings in entitled "The Curse of the lost Adams diggings" and is covered from pages 145-157. Contains the basic Adams account, including the stories of Captain Shaw, Bob Lewis, John Dowling and John Brewer. The section on the Southwest quadrant includes a chapter on treasures of the malpais as well.

--------*Buried Treasures of the American Southwest: Legends of Lost Mines, Hidden Payrolls and Spanish Gold* (August House/Little Rock, 1989) 220 p. As the title suggests, a good collection of treasure tales from Arizona, Arkansas, New Mexico, Oklahoma and Texas. The Lost Adams is one of four entries related to New Mexico covered from pages 123-130.

-------*The Lost Canyon of Gold: Discovering the Legendary Lost Adams Diggings* (TwoDot, 2017) 172 p. Jameson's book is divided into three parts. Part I provides his own pastiche of the legend, and my favorite thing about the book is how Jameson compares Dobie's reconstruction of Adams to the "Hero's Journey" as famously outlined by Jospeh Campbell. This book will be of most interest due to Jameson's claim that he may well have found the canyon via the aid of clairvoyant Jim Peterson. Though it may sound farfetched, Peterson's premonition's of world events were said to come true. Jameson's description of the canyon, complete with waterfall, cabin foundation, and Native American ceremonial grounds, would seem to imply that it may truly be the Lost Adams, or if not Sno-Ta-Hay Canyon itself, a similar canyon. But you can determine that for yourself after reading the book, which I do recommend.

Johnston, Langford. *Old Magdalena Cowtown* (Bandar Log, Inc. 1983) 127 p. The book contains sixteen chapters, a glossary and index of cattle brands plus maps of cattle ranches. The Lost Adams Diggings comprises Chapter 15 starting on page 110 and ending on page 121. Gives a unique account of the diggings which was covered in this book's second chapter.

Kemp, Ben W. and J.C. Dykes. *Cow Dust and Saddle Leather* (University of Oklahoma Press, 1968) 322 p. Chapter 20: "The Adam's Story" contains the account of Washie Jones from pages 267-283. Of interest for Old West enthusiasts in general; also has chapters on the Apache Kid and Black Jack Ketchum among others.

Kutz, Jack. *Mysteries & Miracles of New Mexico* **(Rhombus Publishing Company, 1988) 220 p.** Contains seventeen chapters on strange New Mexico related stories, of which the Adams Diggings is included from pages 21-32. For the most part, Kutz paints his own Dobie-esque pastiche of the diggings, but also adds in some interesting bits at the end per gold discoveries on the New Mexico Navajo reservation.

McKenna, James A. *Black Range Tales* **(The Rio Grande Press, 1936/1984) 306 p.** The section of the book entitled "Lost Canyon Diggings" comprises pages 30-76. The firsthand account of Jason Baxter's return to the Adams Diggings is probably the most interesting thing about the book. It's become, in its own strange way, more credible than the Adams version in that there's at least less contradictions whereas Baxter is concerned. It also, of course, presents its own take on the Adams tale, plus much, much more.

Mitchell, John D. *Lost Mines of the Great Southwest* **(The Rio Grande Press, Inc., 1933/1970) 180 p.** Contains a four page entry on the Lost Adams Diggings. Notably it connects the journal entries of Robert T. Emmet and also the notes of Lieutenant W.H. Emory with the legend of Adams.

Penfield, Thomas. *Dig Here! Lost Mines & Buried Treasure of the Southwest* **(Adventures Unlimited Press, 1962/2004) 240 p.** Overall this book can be recommended to treasure enthusiasts, as it is fairly exhaustive in the amount of ground it covers. Oddly, Penfield doesn't include the traditional Adams Diggings tale as an entry at all. Although his chapter is listed as "Lost Adams Diggings," it is all on the discovery of a cave of gold on an Arizona Navajo reservation by an Indian trader named Henry Adams. Penfield notes that the two legends were often confused for one another, but what's even more confusing is how the Southwest's greatest treasure yarn wasn't properly included in Penfield's book at all.

Purcell, Jack. *The Lost Adams Diggings: Myth, Mystery and Madness* **(Nine Lives Press, 2003) 240 p.** If I were to set out to write the end-all-be-all book on the Lost Adams, I would have structured it much like Jack Purcell did. What I love about the book is that Purcell reprints all of the original source material on the Adams, sans and pre-dating Dobie, I might clarify. Basically, accounts like Byerts are reprinted in full so you can read them for yourself with Purcell adding insightful footnotes. Said footnotes typically either point out how one account contradicts another, or how the account matches up well with another account and proven history, locations, etc. Though Dobie originated the myth, I feel like Purcell does the best job of actually panning for the truth. If you could read only one book on the subject, I would pick this one. Unfortunately, the edition I purchased has no page numbers, which I assume might be a one off mistake.

Randle, Kevin D. *Lost Gold & Buried Treasure: A Treasure Hunter's Guide to 250 Fortunes Waiting to be Found* (M. Evans & Company, Inc., 1995) 302 p. Kevin D. Randle, best known as one of the first ufologists to take a deep dive into the Roswell Incident, is the author of this treasure tome. Randal based most of his Lost Adams accounts on Dobie and the *El Paso Herlad* articles of the 1920s, which is what thankfully led me to the very intriguing accounts of Alvin D. Hudson. The diggings serve as the book's first chapter from pages 13-36. Among many of the Adams related books, this one offers fairly unique information.

Reynolds, Ralph. *Die Rich Here* (Trafford, 2012) 152 p. Of the newer books on the Adams, this is one of the best. The author grew up in the Mogollon region and launched his own search for the diggings. Among other things it led to a man named John D. Adams, who claimed to be a descendant of John R. Adams, who had owned a freighting company, left his family behind, and disappeared out West after finding a gold mine in the 1860s. (This actually lines up rather well with the account given to Langford Johnston, who said Adams left a family behind and was named John H. Adams.) Also includes several stories of similar finds in the area. Lots of good stuff overall.

Simmons, Marc. *Treasure Trails of the Southwest* **(University of New Mexico Press, 1994) 163 p.** Chapter 18: "The Lost Adams Diggings" is included on pp.92-97 and gives the basic accounts of Adams and Brewer per Dobie, though Simmons at least noted that Dobie's version was a pastiche. The book will be of interest to Adams hunters not for the Adams chapter, but for related entries such as "The Lost Gold of San Rafael" and "Treasures of the Pinos Altos" among others.

Thompson, Jerry D. *Under the Piñon Tree: Finding a Place in Pie Town* **(University of New Mexico Press, 2023) 268 p.** Thompson's boyhood reminiscences of Pie Town in the 1940s and 1950s includes his memory of the Adams legend from pages 178-181. Also of note are a few bits on the nearby Adams Diggings post office and its founders.

Tietjen, Gary L. *Encounter with the Frontier* **(1969) 133 p.** A narrative of McKinley County, New Mexico, it includes its own rendition of the diggings, which Richard French mentioned in *Four Days from Fort Wingate*, though I have never been able to find a copy for myself.

Valley-Fox, Anne and Ann Lacy (Compilers). *Lost Treasures & Old Mines: A New Mexico Federal Writers' Project Book* **(Sunstone Press, 2011) 266 p.** This collection of Federal Writer's Project interviews is an excellent reference source for Adams enthusiasts, probably more so for tales on related events and gold caches. Contains two main entries on the Adams Diggings, one of which changed it to the singular "Adam's Diggings," and the other account is that of E.V. Batchler who also recounts the story that Bob Lewis told him.

Additional Sources

Books

Ball, Eve with Nora Henn and Lynda A. Sanchez. *Indeh: An Apache Odyssey.* University of Oklahoma Press, 1988 (second edition).

Connor, Daniel Ellis. *Joseph Reddeford Walker and the Arizona Adventure*. University of Oklahoma Press, 2016.

Cochise, Niño. *The First Hundred Years of Nino Cochise (The Untold Story of an Apache Indian Chief)*. Pyramid Books, 1972.

Dobie, J. Frank. *Apache Gold & Yaqui Silver*. Little, Brown and Company, 1939.

Raynor, Ted. *Old Timers Talk in Southwestern New Mexico*. Texas Western Press, 1960.

Robinson, Sherry. *Apache Voices: Their Stories of Survival as Told to Eve Ball*. University of New Mexico Press, 2000.

Articles
Baily, Horace. "Treasure of Massacre Mine." *True Western Adventure* (February 1959).

Dillon, George. "Apache Gold." *Gold!* (Annual, 1969).

Galbraith, Den. "The Lost Ledge of Governor Otero." *True West* (March-April 1964).

King, Austin T. "Nana's Gold." (Publication unknown)

Phillips, Jerry. "A Pilot's Opinion of the Lost Adams." *Gold!* (Fall 1975).

Whitehouse, Stuart. "Charlie Adams and the Valley of Gold." *Golden West* (November 1964).

INDEX

ABOUT THE AUTHOR

John LeMay was born and raised in Roswell, NM, the "UFO Capital of the World." He is the author of over 50 books, many of them on the history of the Southwest such as *Tall Tales and Half Truths of Billy the Kid*, and *Roswell USA: Towns That Celebrate UFOs, Lake Monsters, Bigfoot and Other Weirdness*. In addition to non-fiction, he is also the author of the novels *The Noted Desperado Pancho Dumez* and *Once Upon a Time in Fort Sumner*. He is also the editor/publisher of *Strange West Magazine* and has written for Western journals and magazines such as *True West*, *The Coalition Journal*, the *Tombstone Epitaph*, and the *Wild West History Association Journal*. He is a Past President of the Board of Directors for the Historical Society for Southeast New Mexico.

The following titles are available for purchase on Amazon.com, and are available to bookstores at a wholesale discount via Ingram Content Group (ISBNs of available editions listed for this purpose)

CRYPTOZOOLOGY/COWBOYS & SAURIANS

Cowboys & Saurians: Prehistoric Beasts as Seen by the Pioneers explores dinosaur sightings from the pioneer period via real newspaper reports from the time. Well-known cases like the Tombstone Thunderbird are covered along with more obscure cases like the Crosswicks Monster and more. Softcover (357 pp/5.06" X 7.8") Suggested Retail: $19.95 ISBN: 978-1-7341546-1-0

Cowboys & Saurians: Ice Age zeroes in on snowbound saurians like the Ceratosaurus of the Arctic Circle and a Tyrannosaurus of the Tundra, as well as sightings of Ice Age megafauna like mammoths, glyptodonts, Sarkastodons and Sabertoothed tigers. Tales of a land that time forgot in the Arctic are also covered. Softcover (264 pp/5.06" X 7.8") Suggested Retail: $14.99 ISBN: 978-1-7341546-7-2

Southerners & Saurians takes the series formula of exploring newspaper accounts of monsters in the pioneer period with an eye to the Old South. In addition to dinosaurs are covered Lizardmen, Frogmen, giant leeches and mosquitoes, and the Dingocroc, which might be an alien rather than a prehistoric survivor. Softcover (202 pp/5.06" X 7.8") Suggested Retail: $13.99 ISBN: 978-1-7344730-4-9

Cowboys & Saurians South of the Border explores the saurians of Central and South America, like the Patagonian Plesiosaurus that was really an Iemisch, plus tales of the Neo-Mylodon, a menacing monster from underground called the Minhocao, Glyptodonts, and even Bolivia's three-headed dinosaur! Softcover (412 pp/5.06"X7.8") Suggested Retail: $17.95 ISBN: 978-1-953221-73-5

UFOLOGY/THE REAL COWBOYS & ALIENS IN CONJUNCTION WITH ROSWELL BOOKS

The Real Cowboys and Aliens: Early American UFOs explores UFO sightings in the USA between the years 1800-1864. Stories of encounters sometimes involved famous figures in U.S. history such as Lewis and Clark, and Thomas Jefferson.Hardcover (242pp/6" X 9") Softcover (262 pp/5.06" X 7.8") Suggested Retail: $24.99 (hc)/$15.95(sc) ISBN: 978-1-7341546-8-9\(hc)/978-1-7344730-8-7(sc)

The second entry in the series, *Old West UFOs*, covers reports spanning the years 1865-1895. Includes tales of Men in Black, Reptilians, Spring-Heeled Jack, Sasquatch from space, and other alien beings, in addition to the UFOs and airships. Hardcover (276 pp/6" X 9") Softcover (308 pp/5.06" X 7.8") Suggested Retail: $29.95 (hc)/$17.95(sc) ISBN: 978-1-7344730-0-1 (hc)/ 978-1-73447 30-2-5 (sc)

The third entry in the series, *The Coming of the Airships*, encompasses a short time frame with an incredibly high concentration of airship sightings between 1896-1899. The famous Aurora, Texas, UFO crash of 1897 is covered in depth along with many others. Hardcover (196 pp/6" X 9") Softcover (222 pp/5.06" X 7.8") Suggested Retail: $24.99 (hc)/$15.95(sc) ISBN: 978-1-7347816 -1-8 (hc)/978-1-7347816-0-1(sc)

Featuring cases the authors missed, *The Lost Cases* covers things such as the skyquakes recorded by Lewis and Clark, airships and the Spanish American War, Pancho Villa and crystal skulls, lost alien tribe of the Tundra, invisible alien monsters, the Great Moon Hoax of 1835, hellhounds and airships, the Sonora Airship Club and more. Softcover (252 pp/5.06" X 7.8") Suggested Retail: $18.99 ISBN: 978-1-953221-55-1

Cowboys & Saurians: Dinosaurs Down Under takes the series to Australia to explore tales of the cattle devouring Burrunjor, the dreaded Diprotodon, the terrible Tantanoola Tiger, the marsupial Sasquatch known as the Yowie, plus Thylacines, Bunyips, giant rabbits, Megalodons and dinosaurs in nearby New Zealand. Softcover (240 pp/ 5.06" X 7.8") Suggested Retail: $14.95 ISBN: 978-1-953221-34-6

As the title suggest, *Cowboys & Saurians in the Modern Era* takes the series into the 20th Century with tales of the Texas Pterosaur flap of 1976, the Bladenboro Beast of the 1950s, the Busco Turtle Beast of the 1940s, dinosaur sightings in the Great Depression and far out tales of mini-mastodons, dinosaur men, and Snallygasters. Softcover (320 pp/ 5.06" X 7.8") Suggested Retail: $19.95 ISBN: 978-1-953221-22-3

Settlers & Serpents wrangles the best "Snaik Stories" of the Southwest and beyond in a single volume. Whether it's simple giant snakes or lake serpents, they're corralled in the pages within. Also included are entries on the Leviathan in Mesoamerica and the Southwest plus a detailed look at the giant rattlesnake of Pecos Pueblo. Softcover (180 pp/ 5.06" X 7.8") Suggested Retail: $14.99 ISBN: 978-1-953221-21-6

Written for young readers *Monsters of the Old South* collects the best creature stories of the swamplands including the White River Monster, Green Eyes, the Crocodingo, the Averasboro Gallinipper, the Tennessee Snake Woman, the Arkansas Gowrow, Bigfoot in the Mississippi River and more. Softcover (122 pp/4.25" X 7") Suggested Retail: $12.99 ISBN: 978-17347816-9-4

Early 20th Century UFOs kicks off a new series that investigates UFO sightings of the early 1900s. Includes tales of UFOs sighted over the *Titanic* as it sunk, Nikola Tesla receiving messages from the stars, an alien being found encased in ice, and a possible virus from outer space!Hardcover (196 pp/6" X 9") Softcover (222 pp/5.06" X 7.8") Suggested Retail: $27.99 (hc)/$16.95(sc) ISBN: 978-1-7347816-1-8 (hc)/978-1-73478 16-0-1(sc)

UFOs in the Roaring Twenties takes a look at UFO sightings in the 1920s just as the title suggests, along with accounts of Mothman in Nebraska, Lincoln LaPaz's first UFO case, Men in Black investigating an airship crash in Braxton County, West Virginia, Camden's Cosmic Sniper, and much more! Softcover (248 pp/5.06" X 7.8") Suggested Retail: $19.99 ISBN: 978-1-953221-51-3

UFOs of the Turbulent Thirties concludes the authors' investigation of the last unexplored decade of Ufology in the Great Depression with accounts of Mothman, Ghost Fliers, Nazi Bells, the Underground City of the Lizard People, a vanished village on the tundra, and even gangsters and aliens. Softcover (212 pp/5.06" X 7.8") Suggested Retail: $17.95 ISBN: 978-1-953221-35-3

Written for young readers ages 9-12, *Space Monsters of the Old West* collects the best alien sightings of the Wild West including Mummies from Mars, Bigfoot from the Moon, Pascagoula's space ghouls, the Crawfordsville Monster, Spring-Heeled Jack, Blobs from space, and even the dinosaurian alien creatures that invaded Van Meter, Iowa. Softcover (120 pp/4.25" X 7") Suggested Retail: $12.99 ISBN: 978-1-953221-87-2

COWBOYS & MONSTERS

Cowboys & Monsters features potentially true stories of real vampires, werewolves, and even mummies unique to America's Wild West period. Examples include the cursed mummy of John Wilkes Booth, New Orleans immortal vampire Jacques St. Germain, precursors to the Beast of Bray Road, and the origins of Skinwalker Ranch. Softcover (316 pp/5.06" X 7.8") Suggested Retail: $19.99 ISBN: 978-1-953221-46-9

The first entry in this trilogy of non-fiction terror sinks its teeth into the lore of the vampire in North America and Mexico, with detailed rundowns on the vampire hunters of Exeter, Rhode Island, a tribe of Bat People, the nocturnal shape-shifting vampire witches of Tlaxcala, and the immortal ways of Comte St. Germain in New Orleans and more. Softcover (200 pp/ 5.06" X 7.8") Suggested Retail: $12.99 ISBN: 978-1-953221-38-4

Mummies of the Americas explores Death Valley's city of the Dead, King Tut's Tomb along the Arkansas, the Egyptian City of the Grand Canyon plus the famous mummies of John Wilkes Boothe, Elmer McCurdy, the Cardiff Giant, the Mummy of Helldorado, and even Billy the Kid's pickled trigger finger! Softcover (200 pp/5.06" X 7.8") Suggested Retail: $12.99 ISBN: 978-1-953221-37-7

Cowboys & Dogmen is devoted to tales of werewolves of the Wild West including the dreaded Navajo skinwalker, the Watrous Werewolf, the Beast of the Land Between Lakes, the Hellhounds of El Dorado Canyon, the dreaded Dog Eater, the Wahhoo, the Wolf Man of Versailles, the Michigan Dog-Man and more! Softcover (212 pp/5.06" X 7.8") Suggested Retail: $12.99 ISBN: 978-1-953221-36-0

FICTION/ MISC. HISTORY

The first novel from historian John LeMay weaves a fantastic web of fiction via real life mysteries and legends of New Mexico, namely the puzzling theft and return of Billy the Kid's tombstone in 1976, the legend of the Lost Adams Diggings, the villainous Santa Fe Ring, and the enigmatic Acoma Mesa. Softcover (250 pp/5.5" X 7.5") Suggested Retail: $14.95 ISBN: 978-1-953221-42-1

The year is 1950, and old timers connected to the long-dead outlaw Billy the Kid are turning up murdered in New Mexico. Some blame the killings on the avenging witch of the Navajo nation, the skinwalker, while others think it's no coincidence that a man claiming to be a surviving Billy the Kid is set to meet with the governor soon... Softcover (260 pp/5.5" X 7.5") Suggested Retail: $16.95 ISBN: 978-1-953221-32-2

Roswell, USA, the long-forgotten debut work of John LeMay, is available again and covers the minutia of the infamous Roswell UFO Crash of 1947. Notable chapters include tales of an alien ghost haunting the old airbase, monsters in the nearby Bottomless Lakes, and even a dinosaur sighting outside of town. Softcover (248 pp/6" X 9") Suggested Retail: $14.95 ISBN: 978-0-9817597-5-3

This biography, for the first time ever, tells the history of western journalist Ash Upson, who ghostwrote Pat Garrett's *The Authentic Life of Billy the Kid* in 1882 and also reproduces many of Upson's letters that detailed the harsh realities of frontier life in New Mexico during the turbulent Lincoln County War. Softcover (318 pp/5.5" X 8.5") Suggested Retail: $16.99 ISBN: 978-1953221919

185

From the author of *Legend & Lore of the Lost Adams Diggings*

LOST ADAMS COUNTRY
Hidden Treasures of Apacheria

JOHN LEMAY

www.ingramcontent.com/pod-product-compliance
Lightning Source LLC
Chambersburg PA
CBHW061330120626
46546CB00007B/2744